American Red Cross Instructor Candidate Training Participant's Manual

American Red Cross

Contents

Preface

This course, sanctioned by the Board of Governors by resolution at the 1987 National Convention, accommodates cross training between Health and Safety, Disaster, and other services and combines entry-level training for Red Cross instructors.

The Instructor Candidate Training (ICT) course was developed to serve as a prerequisite for a number of Red Cross instructor training courses. It is training in which Red Cross paid and volunteer staff learn fundamental teaching skills. The training is managed by a Red Cross unit (the chapter, military station, operations headquarters, or national headquarters).

It is hoped that all new instructor candidates will capture the excitement of teaching and experience the rewards of helping others learn. In the American Red Cross, it is especially meaningful to be engaged in teaching information that saves lives and alleviates suffering.

The American Red Cross Instructor Candidate Training course was designed and developed as a collaborative effort by paid and volunteer staff. Primary writers were—

Betsy Ratcliff, chairman, Chapter Services, Western West Virginia Chapter, Huntington, West Virginia.

Stephen Silverman, Ed.D., The University of Texas at Austin; Centex Chapter, Austin, Texas; and national volunteer consultant, Health and Safety Development, national headquarters, Washington, D.C.

Mary Ann Hankin, Ed.D., Human Resources, national headquarters, Washington, D.C.

Members of the Development Committee who gave direction to the design were—

Ann E. Bartholomew, Disaster Services, national headquarters, Washington, D.C.

Jane Brooks Mays, CFRE, Office of Financial Development, Eastern Operations Headquarters, Alexandria, Virginia.

Christopher Saeger, Disaster Services, national headquarters, Washington, D.C.

Jean Wagaman, Health and Safety, national headquarters, Washington, D.C.

Recognition is given to the following individuals for their contributions to the evaluation process:

Diane Davis, Ph.D.,volunteer, Prince Georges County Chapter, Hyattsville, Maryland

Rocky Lopes, Ph.D., Disaster Services, national headquarters, Washington, D.C.

Sharron Silva, Ph.D., Programs and Services, national headquarters, Washington, D.C.

The Oversight Committee, handling major policy and philosophical issues relating to the system, had the following representatives from the participating services and offices:

Kathleen Curry, Disaster Services, national headquarters, Washington, D.C.

Kathryn Doyle, Programs and Services, national headquarters, Washington, D.C.

Imogene Huffman, Human Resources, national headquarters, Washington, D.C.

Kathleen King, Public Support, national headquarters, Washington, D.C.

John Malatak, Ph.D., Health and Safety, national headquarters, Washington, D.C.

Appreciation is given to the following Red Cross chapters that provided field test sites and instructor trainers to conduct the tests and to those chapters engaged in pilot tests:

Cincinnati Area Chapter, Cincinnati, Ohio

Dallas Area Chapter, Dallas, Texas

Napa Chapter, Napa, California

Nashville Area Chapter, Nashville, Tennessee

Prince Georges County Chapter, Hyattsville, Maryland

Santa Clara Valley Chapter, San Jose, California

Tulsa Area Chapter, Tulsa, Oklahoma

Western West Virginia Chapter, Huntington, West Virginia

Appreciation is also extended to all of the reviewers, field test observers, and instructor trainers who provided meaningful input into the course design.

Acknowledgment is given to Zenger-Miller, Inc., for permission to adapt its instructor guide format and to Career Systems, Inc., for permission to use its Career Development Model in the videocassette section on teaching methods.

Unit 1: Introducing the Course

Unit 1: Introducing the Course

Purpose of This Manual

The purpose of the *Instructor Candidate Training Participant's Manual* is twofold.

- To supplement the Instructor Candidate Training course.
- To serve as a reference manual when an instructor prepares to teach a Red Cross course. This manual is an integral part of instructor specialty training, the specific training needed to teach a Red Cross specialty course, e.g., American Red Cross Community CPR.

Role of Training

American Red Cross instructors make a difference in their communities by teaching people lifesaving skills, infant and child care skills, healthier lifestyles, and recreational safety and disaster relief skills, to name a few. Red Cross instructors also teach specific Red Cross career enhancement and management skills, such as fund-raising methods.

Red Cross Mission

Instructors are committed to a cause—to promote the mission of the American Red Cross, which is to improve the quality of human life; to enhance self-reliance and concern for others; and to help people avoid, prepare for, and cope with emergencies.

Instructor Responsibilities

An American Red Cross instructor has certain responsibilities. The instructor—

1. Plans to teach, conducts, and evaluates a course.
2. Evaluates participants' eligibility for course completion certificates.
3. Maintains complete, accurate course reports and records.
4. Demonstrates appropriate qualities as a Red Cross representative and role model.

Steps in the Instructor Training Process

A four-step process has been designed to prepare instructors. The steps in this process are—

1. *Completion of instructor specialty course prerequisites.* The requirements for courses vary. They include taking the specialty course and may include minimum age; experience

with the subject matter; and/or ability to perform a particular skill, such as cardiopulmonary resuscitation (CPR). The prerequisites may be completed before or after successful completion of the ICT course.

2. *Successful completion of the Instructor Candidate Training (ICT)* course. Criteria for completing this course are meeting the objectives through—

   ● Attendance at all sessions.

   ● A passing score of 80 percent or higher on the written test.

   ● Participation in task assignments and other learning activities.

3. *Successful completion of an instructor specialty course.* The instructor specialty course is a course in which instructor candidates learn how to teach a specific course. Some instructor specialty courses include written tests, in addition to skills performance review and/or practice teaching sessions.

4. *Receiving certification and authorization.* Certification is the formal recognition given after successful completion of a Red Cross course. Authorization is the endorsement or permission to teach given by the authorizing Red Cross unit in which the instructor will be teaching.

For Health and Safety and Human Resources instructors in the decentralized plan, authorization comes from the local Red Cross unit. For Financial Development instructors, approval is required from the operations headquarters of jurisdiction. For Disaster Services instructor authorization information, see *Disaster Training System* (ARC 3065).

Instructor Cross Training

In the Red Cross, training of instructors previously trained in one discipline to teach in another discipline is called cross training. Once you have been authorized to teach a course, for example, Introduction to Disaster Services, you may wish to become cross trained to teach a course in Health and Safety, such as Standard First Aid. Cross training is accomplished by—

1. Meeting instructor specialty course prerequisites, including taking the course.

2. Receiving approval from the new Red Cross service.

3. Successfully completing the instructor specialty course.

4. Receiving certification and authorization.

Unit 2: Understanding Students and the Learning Process

Unit 2: Understanding Students and the Learning Process

There are a number of theories about the learning process and styles of learning. Knowledge of a few basic concepts of learning theory will assist you in helping your students to learn.

The Learning Process

Learning can be defined as a process of change through which people acquire new knowledge, skills, or attitudes as a result of some type of study or experience. Learning occurs over time and should be considered a lifelong process or experience. If change of some kind does not occur, the teaching is ineffective. As an instructor, you motivate students to acquire new information, remember it, and apply it. But students must do the learning, and they learn best by being involved in the learning experience.

Types of Learning in Red Cross Courses

Red Cross courses include three types of learning. They are—

- Cognitive: Facts, concepts, application skills. Facts and concepts are taught and students are provided opportunities to apply the information (interviewing a disaster victim, approaching an accident scene, raising funds, etc.).

- Affective: Attitudes as they affect behavior. Red Cross courses also can help people examine attitudes that affect behavior and change attitudes that may result in undesirable behavior. Examples include courses examining food preferences, concerns about HIV/AIDS transmission, or sensitivity toward the feelings of individuals in need of disaster assistance.

- Psychomotor: Motor skills. Many Red Cross courses teach skills that combine thought and physical action. Such courses include swimming and taking blood pressures.

Many Red Cross courses include all three types of learning. Teaching methods used for each type of learning are discussed in Unit 4, Conducting a Course.

Motivation to Learn
Learners go through decision-making steps before beginning a learning project or course. One step is to make a decision about what they want to learn.

Reasons people take Red Cross courses vary, but may include—

- Job skills: Lifeguarding, disaster, and fund-raising courses and advancement or leadership courses. Students taking these courses are likely to be highly motivated.

- Support of safe leisure-time activities: Canoeing, swimming, sailing courses. Most students in these courses are motivated, as this is likely something they want to do.

- Life problems or changes: Stress management and health care courses for older adults and infants. Students are likely to be highly motivated to learn to help themselves or others.

- General interest: First aid and CPR courses. Student motivation is usually high.

- Self-improvement: Career counseling and writing courses. High motivation is usually evident.

- External requirement for certification: CPR or first aid courses. This reason might include taking a course as a job requirement. Motivation depends on how badly students want or need certification.

Learning, a Social Process
In American Red Cross courses, people are taught in groups and learn from reading, watching videos, observing others, listening to opinions or facts, or participating in group activities. The learning outcomes are that individuals accept change and share experiences. Within these groups, people will come with different ideas and needs. Since learning is a process of change, students may need help in accepting change.

Accepting Change
The objective of learning is to replace or enhance some of the ways we think or act with new ideas, attitudes, or behaviors. But people differ in the way they accept change. Some people may become anxious when they are expected to perform new skills or to be tested on new knowledge. They may try to reduce their anxiety by holding on to familiar ways of thinking and doing things.

Consider what learning objectives might trigger anxiety. For example, learning new motor skills that require a high degree of coordination may cause anxiety. This is true since poor performance is obvious to other group members and could cause personal embarrassment. Giving students an opportunity to talk about old and new behaviors in a supportive, positive environment will help them in accepting new information.

Sharing Experiences
Students need to feel free to share their first attempts in expressing new ideas or in performing new activities. Adults who have been away from the classroom for some time, especially if they did not like school, may find it harder to take risks and to share their ideas with others in the class. Providing support and encouragement and being positive will help them to be more relaxed and open in the learning environment.

Part of learning also may involve making mistakes. Help students to understand that few people do everything right the first time they try. Support, encouragement, and corrective feedback (discussed in Unit 3, Being an Effective Instructor) will help motivate students to continue the learning process by sharing with others.

Learning Differences   People learn things in different ways and at different speeds. Teaching methods need to accommodate these differences when possible. One way is to find out who is having difficulty learning. You can do this by asking questions, by observing, and by encouraging students to ask questions. A student who learns quickly or who enters the course knowing many of the skills that you are teaching may be paired with a student who learns more slowly.

The ways people prefer to learn may differ; some students will want a lot of direction from you, while others will want little direction. Some students are more visual learners, others learn better by listening or by using their kinesthetic sense (awareness of the body and its movement). Generally, a student will learn and remember better when instruction fits his or her learning style. You may not be able to know your students beforehand or determine their learning preferences; however, using a variety of teaching methods will help you more closely meet different learning preferences.

Physical Environment

The physical environment may have an important effect on learning. Ideally learning takes place in an environment as free as possible from factors that interfere with learning. For example, your most effective teaching efforts could be hindered if students are too hot or too cold.

The following environmental factors are important for you to consider when teaching any course:

- Location of the class (chapter classroom, business conference room, etc.)
- Size of class (generally between 6 and 20 participants)
- Class setting (acoustics, lighting, temperature, wall colors, and clutter)
- Interruptions or distractions (noise, weather, and the frequent movement of people or objects)

Depending on the situation and the student, many of the above factors can enhance or inhibit learning.

As a Red Cross instructor, you may find that you will be teaching in a variety of locations. Some will be more conducive to learning than others. You may teach in multipurpose rooms; classrooms; conference rooms; and, depending on the course, outdoors. Some courses will be at Red Cross chapters, while others may be at business or industrial locations. However, it is important to check the location as early as possible to determine if there are any changes that need to be or can be made. A positive, comfortable class environment will help increase the motivation to learn and make your teaching more successful.

The size of the class, if too small, provides little opportunity for sharing and peer support. If the class is too large, the size may discourage some students from offering comments or asking questions and also may not allow for individual attention that is needed.

Poor acoustics and lighting, distracting wall colors or decorations, and clutter are factors that can detract from learning. Choosing a classroom that is removed from noise and other interruptions and distractions will help facilitate learning. Some things you have control over, but at times you will have to make the best of situations that are less than ideal.

In summary, before students can learn, they must be motivated to learn. They need to feel free to learn in their own way and at their own pace, when possible. The attitude of you, the instructor, is crucial in this process. Recognition of students' learning differences and trying to meet their needs will help to facilitate their learning.

Concepts of Learning

Four concepts about learning will help you in teaching Red Cross courses. They are motivation, association, repetition, and use of the senses.

Motivation
Students need to understand the worth of a subject and be motivated and ready to learn. Most students who take a Red Cross course are motivated to learn from the start because for them learning is goal directed—acquiring new information for a job or satisfying other needs. Effective learning does not occur without motivation. As an instructor, you need to look for ways to enhance or maintain students' motivation to learn.

Knowing each student by name and understanding each student's reason for coming to the class are important steps in increasing motivation. Knowing your students can help you to be specific in referring certain ideas to a student's situation. Knowing your students helps you find personal references that may help less motivated students find reasons to learn. Give students recognition and respect by treating each as an individual and respecting each individual's values. By doing this, you can positively influence their self-esteem and motivation for learning.

Association
It is easier to learn something new if the material builds on information already learned or on previous experiences. Association helps students understand that what they already know can help them in learning something new. It also helps them to recall the new information when they need it. An example of association is the mnemonic MARS (motivation, association, repetition, and senses). (A mnemonic is something

that aids the memory.) MARS is formed from the first letters of the four concepts of learning. Through association, MARS helps students remember the concepts of learning.

Repetition

Repetition should occur as quickly as possible after any new information is given. Review of material and practice of skills help students learn. However, it needs to be at the appropriate level of the learner. In addition, students need to know how they are doing. Prompt and accurate feedback tells them whether they have performed correctly and how to improve their performance. Repetition needs to include corrective feedback and structured practice. Unstructured practice or repetition itself may result in learning incorrect information or skills.

Use of the Senses

Learning takes place more easily when more than one sense is involved—seeing, hearing, smelling, tasting, and feeling (both by touch and through the kinesthetic sense). The senses are a channel or connection to new information—a large percentage of which is gained through sight.

Using as many senses as possible reinforces learning and helps students remember. For example, you use several senses in learning CPR. You look at videotapes, you read the manual, and you listen to the instructor. If students hear, see, and do, they are likely to learn more than if they only use one sense. When we teach, the more senses we use the more we help meet students' different learning styles.

Learning occurs best when students are actively involved in the learning process. Learning is retained for a much shorter period of time when the learner is passive—listening—than when the learner is actively involved.

Student Characteristics

Student characteristics include education, reading ability, and language; experiences; coordination, strength, and size; attitude; and health and physical fitness. Your teaching will be more effective if you learn as much about your students as possible before the course begins. (See Appendix G: Managing Diversity to Enhance the Learning Process.)

Education, Reading Ability, Language

Research shows that the higher the level of education obtained, the more motivated students are to learn and to seek out new learning experiences. Educational level also is important because most Red Cross courses require reading. If students read at a level that is significantly below the reading level of the standard course material, you may have to provide these students with an outline of major course ideas and an overview of key words and concepts to support them in reading the course material. These students may benefit if ideas are illustrated by examples taken from their own experiences and knowledge. In addition, the use of oral rather than written tests may help students with low reading ability demonstrate what they have learned.

If English is a second language or there are other language barriers (for example, a course taught in a Spanish dialect different from the student's dialect), you may have to consider using additional devices to promote learning (more audiovisuals, slower presentations) and asking frequent questions to be sure that students understand you. (Your authorizing unit may be able to provide a translator or materials in the language.) Assessing the students and their background and abilities will greatly assist in helping students to learn.

Experiences

Each student has had a variety of experiences during his or her lifetime. Learning may be enhanced if instructors know what experiences students have to draw on for examples and to build on as new information is given. Students often enjoy recounting their experiences once they are comfortable in the classroom setting. This can increase motivation for other students. Long stories that are only partly related to the topic or too many stories should be discouraged.

Coordination, Strength, Size

Coordination, strength, and size will affect a student's ability to perform certain skills. For example, strength and stamina may be important factors for success in performing skills that involve the use of heavy equipment or in mastering some of the more complex swimming strokes. Also, some skills demand levels of coordination that may be beyond the physical ability of some students.

Identifying such limitations early and observing students closely during practice sessions will help you determine how these situations can be handled. You may need to encourage some students to devote more time to practice; others need to be apprised of the situation and directed toward goals that are within their capabilities. Those who will be teaching psychomotor skills will get more information in the specialty courses.

Attitude

A student's attitude affects learning. Individuals who are outgoing often are the easiest to motivate. Students with a negative attitude are more difficult to motivate and less effective learners. Students who are upset or distressed may also be difficult to teach. For example, a student is requested by his employer to attend the course, but he did not want to come, or a student had a previous bad experience in a course. Finding out as much as you can about students before and during a course will help you to identify attitude problems and will give you an opportunity to help students overcome them.

Health and Physical Fitness

You need to be alert if any of your students are fatigued, ill, or physically impaired. Some students may need to be excused from participating in certain activities. Depending on the course, students may need to be given the opportunity to make up what they missed.

Also keep in mind that many adults have full-time jobs. They may tire easily or already be tired when they come to class—especially if they come to class after working all day—or they may be less responsive or energetic students. To help overcome fatigue, use more audiovisuals, actively involve students in discussions or other activities, and give more frequent "stand up" breaks.

Students who are physically impaired may need additional attention to meet learning objectives. No person shall be deprived of Red Cross service because of his or her color, sex, race, religious beliefs, national origin, or physical or mental handicap as described in the Rehabilitation Act of 1973, except where any individual's safety will, in the opinion of the Red Cross, be adversely affected by the participation of a disabled individual in a Red Cross course.

In summary, instruction needs to be paced to the maturity, education, experience, and ability of the students. Having looked at the learning process and student characteristics, the next unit will focus on characteristics that can help an instructor teach effectively.

Unit 3: Being an Effective Instructor

Unit 3: Being an Effective Instructor

Your most important role as a Red Cross instructor is to help students learn. For you to accomplish this, you must encourage your students to share the responsibility for learning. Some ways to do this include asking questions, encouraging discussion in class, and encouraging each student to actively participate in course exercises, skills practice, and other activities. You may find when you show confidence in a student's ability to learn that the student actually becomes more confident and performs better. Students tend to perform at the level that you expect them to perform. Your role is particularly important in the first stages of learning when students may feel unsure of themselves. At this early stage, students often need more direction from you.

Characteristics of an Effective Instructor

In this section, you will learn characteristics of an effective Red Cross instructor, which include the following:

- Good communication skills to enhance learning through motivation, association, repetition, and use of the senses
- Knowledge of the subject to reinforce course objectives and enhance learning through motivation, association, and repetition
- Positive attitude to help motivate students by being friendly and enthusiastic and by accepting others as individuals
- Appropriate attire and professional appearance to serve as a motivator and role model
- Patience and flexibility to respond to students' learning needs
- Professional behavior to place importance on your conduct and effectiveness in managing your class to motivate students

Good Communication Skills

To be effective as an instructor, you need communication skills that should include careful listening, speaking clearly in a well-modulated voice, and using reinforcing body language.

Communication is the process of transferring a message from one person to another. The three elements of communication are—

- The sender—the person who gains the attention of the receiver and transmits the message.

- The message—an idea or information.

- The receiver—the person(s) who processes and then responds to the message using the senses and interpreting the meaning of the message based on his or her experience, knowledge, prejudices, needs, and emotions.

Effective communication occurs when the receiver interprets the sender's message exactly as intended. Communication can be verbal or nonverbal.

Verbal Communication
Verbal communication can be spoken, written, or sung. One of your most important teaching tools is your voice. Listed below are several things to consider so that you use your voice to the best advantage. If you have problems in any of these areas, practice and feel free to ask an experienced instructor or other Red Cross staff to assist you in developing effective communication skills.

- *Volume*. Talk loud enough so that the student farthest away can hear you. If the group is small, you may need to tone down your voice. On the other hand, if the group is very large, you may need to amplify your voice with a microphone or loudspeaker. If you have never used a microphone, you should practice with it first. Most microphones work best if you use your normal speaking voice.

- *Rate of Delivery*. Vary your rate of speaking according to the difficulty of the subject and the learning ability of the students. Speaking too quickly can confuse students, especially if the topic is unfamiliar to them. On the other hand, if a subject is relatively simple, too slow a pace may irritate some students. When you are nervous, you may talk faster. Remind yourself to slow down.

- *Pronunciation*. Pronounce or accent each syllable clearly and distinctly. Use pauses, raising and lowering your voice in much the same way that punctuation—commas, periods, and question marks—is used in writing. If you have difficulty using expression to make your sentences easier to understand, practice speaking with a tape recorder or a partner.

- *Clear and Simple Language*. Keep your speech crisp and decisive. Avoid distracting speech patterns such as "umm," "uuh," or "you know." If you tend to use these distractions, make a conscious effort to omit them. Use short sentences, stating your point simply. A point simply stated is a point easily understood. Also remember to use words that are familiar to you and your students.

- *Enthusiasm*. Show enthusiasm, friendliness, and excitment about your subject and the students you are teaching. This helps students feel excited about learning. Enthusiasm is catching!

- *Value-Laden Statements*. A value is a principle, standard, or quality held in esteem by a person. A value-laden statement is one in which you express what values you hold. As you teach, it is important to understand your own values and to recognize that others have values that may differ from yours. Be sensitive to cultural or ethnic differences. Students may become upset if you make statements that conflict with what they value. This, in turn, may affect the way students relate to you and cause a barrier to their learning.

  In teaching, it is better to express an opinion, when it is called for, rather than a value-laden statement. For instance, an opinion offered to the question, "Should a mother breast-feed?" might be, "I found breast-feeding to be very rewarding." The statement, "Breast-feeding is the only thing to do," is a value-laden statement. Value-laden statements should be avoided when teaching Red Cross courses.

- *Mixed Messages*. When you say one thing and then do something different, you are giving a mixed message to your students. For example, to announce that you will gladly answer questions and then allow no time for questions leaves students unsure about your intent. Be conscious of mixed messages and always try to avoid them.

Nonverbal Communication

Facial expressions, posture, body movements, physical appearance, and eye contact can convey a message. Nonverbal communication (actions without words) can accompany the spoken word or can communicate a message alone. The most important example of nonverbal communication is body language.

Body language and expressions convey a message about how you think or feel. The following examples will help you to send important messages to support what you are teaching:

Body Language	Message
• Lean head or body forward	• Willingness to listen
• Smile frequently	• Friendliness
• Maintain good eye contact	• Interest
• Uncross your arms	• Openness
• Lean head or body forward	• Enthusiasm

There also are messages that you do not want to send; therefore, you should be aware of the following body language:

Body Language	Message
• Raise an index finger to lips	• Desire to interrupt
• Become fidgety	• Loss of interest
• Clench your fists	• Frustration
• Frown	• Disapproval
• Fold arms across chest	• Defensiveness
• Point directly at a person	• Superiority
• Lower your head	• Stay away, don't bother me

You also need to be aware that there are cultural differences with body language. The meaning of a gesture in one culture may be very different in another culture.

When teaching, the use of natural body movements or gestures communicate that you are relaxed and well prepared for your presentation. Some nervousness before speaking is normal, something that even seasoned professionals experience. Many instructors feel that if they do not have "butterflies" they are not "up" for the presentation. If you remain nervous as the class progresses, you may hurt your teaching; this nervousness may be picked up by students, making it difficult for them to relax and feel comfortable in the learning environment.

Breathing deeply several times will help you and, consequently, the students to relax. Students are usually supportive and want you to succeed.

Listening skills also are important in communicating with students. In order to be a good listener, you need to give your undivided attention to the student who is speaking, whether it is in a private, one-to-one conversation or in the classroom. Interrupting a speaker is not permissible, but questioning for clarification is encouraged.

Listening attentively reinforces the sense of worth you feel about the students, their comments, and the importance of teaching. Listening helps you assess a student's experience, what he or she is learning, and what his or her concerns are.

Good communication is an essential ingredient of an effective instructor. Good communication skills take practice. Having an observer (or your co-instructor) give you feedback on how well you communicate is a good way to identify weaknesses and strengths in your communication skills.

Knowledge of the Subject

Effective instructors must have thorough knowledge of the course subject matter and keep abreast of developments in the subject. An instructor who knows the course content and design and is prepared tends to be more relaxed and to focus on helping students learn, instead of being concerned about what to say next.

The expectation in most Red Cross courses is that you will keep your knowledge of the subject and teaching skills current. The Red Cross stands ready to assist you in this process through newsletters, updated training materials, and other activities, about which you will learn more from your unit of authorization.

Positive Attitude

In thinking about becoming an instructor, you need to consider how you feel about teaching. If you have an interest in the subject, do you have a desire to share it with students? A positive attitude about teaching and helping students learn is essential to being an effective teacher. Such attitudes as friendliness toward your students, an enthusiasm about teaching students, and a positive attitude about accepting students as individuals are attitudes that help students learn.

Appropriate Attire and Professional Appearance

Your appearance can communicate how you feel about yourself, the Red Cross, and your students. Clothing that is worn out of context may direct attention to you and away from learning. Wear proper clothing for the proper setting. Good grooming and clean, well-fitting clothes or Red Cross uniform project an image of pride in yourself and in the organization you represent. (It is recommended that instructors wear Red Cross identification.)

Patience and Flexibility

Patience and flexibility are instructor qualities that also improve learning because they help to provide a more comfortable environment for learning to take place. If you patiently explain facts and answer questions, you encourage an atmosphere that fosters learning.

When standardized Red Cross practice is used in courses, there is little leeway for flexibility. In disaster courses, for example, it is very important that specific topics be covered in the same way throughout the country, so that people assigned to disaster relief have been taught the same information and thus can function together easily as a team.

In some courses, however, you may find several options for presenting material. If this is the case, assess the best way to meet the students' learning needs. Whenever you teach, it is important to give the impression that you have time to help the student who has a question and that you are flexible (when you can be) in considering various ways to meet students' needs.

Professional Behavior

When you teach, it is important to be professional in the way you conduct yourself and your class. Being professional is being punctual (starting and ending the class on time); being reliable (keeping your commitment to teach a class when you agreed to); being able to manage the class (demonstrating skills that enable learning objectives to be met); and following rules and regulations, such as no smoking in the classroom.

Punctually beginning and ending a class makes a statement that you value your students' time and the subject you teach. If you must run over the allotted time, you should do this only with the approval of the students (and in some circumstances the local unit manager or establishment where you are teaching). Learning will drop sharply when people are expecting to leave and cannot. Likewise, beginning late is frustrating and wastes students' time.

Reliability includes planning ahead, preparing well to teach the course, and arriving early to ensure that everything is in order. Red Cross units expect that instructors will come when they say they will. It is a disservice to the students, to the local Red Cross unit, and, ultimately, to the community if you do not keep your commitment.

To summarize, characteristics of an effective instructor are using good communication skills, having an up-to-date knowledge of the subject, having a positive attitude about teaching and sharing information, having a professional appearance, being patient in helping students learn and flexible (when possible) in meeting course objectives, conducting yourself professionally, and managing the class effectively. As you have more experience teaching, you will develop personally and professionally.

Instructor Functions

Instructor functions facilitate students' learning. When teaching, you will need to engage in the following instructor functions:

- Climate setting
- Assigning tasks
- Bridging
- Intervening
- Summarizing

These functions serve as a means to help you focus on why you are here—to help others learn.

Climate Setting   Climate setting is setting the stage at the beginning of the teaching experience to provide a framework in which effective learning can take place. It includes planning for the course so that the learning environment (classroom, pool area, etc.) has the required equipment and materials. But climate setting goes beyond the physical environment. It also involves planning your teaching strategy in such a way that a positive learning environment is established and maintained throughout the entire course.

At the beginning of the course, there are certain points or steps to follow in setting a good climate.

- Post directions to the classroom, if applicable.
- Have name tents or name tags for students.
- Greet students as they arrive for the course as you would a guest in your home.
- Post a welcome sign with the name of the course to help set the stage and to let students know they are in the right location.
- Have Red Cross identification clearly visible.
- Check to see that participants have registered.
- Show students where to place extra materials or wraps.
- Help students to feel comfortable and indicate you are pleased to have them there. A calm, organized setting reinforces the fact that you are prepared and ready to begin.
- Open the first session by welcoming the students and introducing yourself and your co-instructor (if you have one). If the local unit is acting as host, one of the management staff may do this for you.
- Inform students about restroom facilities, smoking policy, fire exits, lunch arrangements, etc.
- Depending on the course design, have students introduce themselves and include information about what they do and what they hope to get from the course.
- Clarify the purpose and learning outcomes of the course.
- Present an overview of the course, giving students what they will be expected to do to earn a course completion certificate.

Throughout the course, you will want to maintain a climate of openness and one that facilitates learning. Overall, the learning climate should be one in which students openly interact. Learn and use students' names and recognize each student's self-worth. A good climate helps to reinforce motivation.

Assigning Tasks Assigning tasks is an instructor function performed whenever students are asked to do an activity. For example, the task may be an exercise, a game, a case study, or a discussion. Tasks may be done in large or small groups, but, in the Red Cross, they are frequently done in small groups.

The purpose of assigning tasks is to involve students in an activity in which they accomplish an objective. The task will be better understood if several of the senses are used—to see it written or demonstrated and to hear it described.

If tasks involve movement of the class into small groups, have participants move at a time that is not disruptive, before or after instructions are given. Be clear about how group members are to be chosen for small group exercises. Circulate among the groups to ensure that the learning objective is being accomplished. Bring groups back together to share learning through reports and discussion. Assigning tasks may use all of the learning concepts—motivation, association, repetition, and the senses.

Bridging Bridging is linking ideas from one section of the course to another and supports learning by association. It connects ideas and allows for learning to be tied to other ideas and teaching from the known to the unknown.

Bridging helps learners experience a logical progression or flow from one concept to another. This is done by describing ideas that relate to the previous learning experience(s).

The instructor accomplishes this by—
- Recalling with the students what they learned in the previous segment (learning through repetition and use of senses).

- Discussing the outcomes expected from the next topic, including how these segments relate to the objectives (learning by association and use of the senses).
- Posting the course outline or objectives and showing development from the current topic to new sections or units. This allows the class to know where they are in the course (learning by association and use of senses).

Bridging, which may take a few minutes or as long as 5 to 10 minutes, is an important part of the learning process. In teaching Red Cross courses, you generally bridge where there is a change in topics to tie together the concepts and to reinforce the learning. The learning concepts of association, repetition, and use of the senses are involved in bridging.

Intervening Intervening is stepping in during the course to ensure positive learning outcomes. This function is accomplished by—

- Clarifying a point.
- Redirecting, strengthening, or modifying the learning process.
- Keeping the subject on track.
- Helping the class to be more effective as a group.
- Focusing on specific content.
- Focusing on overall accomplishments or outcomes of the group.
- Testing an individual student's knowledge or understanding.
- Providing feedback.
- Providing the opportunity to ventilate feelings.
- Closing a topic when time needs to be managed.

For example, if a discussion starts to lose its focus, the instructor can intervene to guide the group in the desired direction. Training yourself to be sensitive to the reactions of your students gives you the ability to spot an individual who is starting to lead the discussion astray. Try to bring the subject back in focus by telling the class they can discuss that topic at another time. It is not always necessary to be highly directive. Simple suggestions and questions are often enough.

Also, if you talk too long, students may feel they are not getting their fair share of the action and may start their own conversations on the side. Bring them into the discussion by asking them questions about the topic.

Many things can make a student restless—an uncomfortable chair, a lengthy session—but there are ways to recapture attention. You might, for instance, vary the location and type of your presentation. You may need to move closer to the class to recapture attention. Loss of control, however, is not always the fault of the instructor. It may be caused by group fatigue. Watch for this and, if necessary, have the class take a break.

Whatever you do, don't let yourself be thrown off balance by a student or a situation. A student's attitude, for example, is sometimes shaped by personal circumstances that have nothing to do with what is going on in the classroom. You have to rely on your good judgment, common sense, and skill as an instructor, keeping in mind that you don't want to embarrass or offend a student. If you plan to use team teaching, discuss interventions candidly with your co-instructor. Together you can decide on ways intervention can be used to avoid any conflicts in the classroom.

This section concentrates on interventions focused on individuals, on the group process, on feedback, and on content.

Focused on the Individual
The talker. Talkative students are often so wrapped up in what they are saying that they don't even realize the effect they are having on others. No one should be given free rein to monopolize the conversation.

One way to discourage the talker is to throw out questions to the other students to bring them into the discussion. Tell the talker, "You've raised a good point." Then turn to the class and add, "Now what do the rest of you think about it?"

The know-it-all. Here is the student who, by virtue of having considerable experience, intelligence, or position, frequently knows the right answer and all too frequently wants to share it.

Sometimes, however, the know-it-all may only be a self-styled expert.

In any case, the know-it-all should be reminded that the opinions of others are important too. You may be able to do this by tactfully addressing questions to other students. Or you can take the know-it-all aside during the break or after class. For example, say, "You had some good points to offer today; it shows you're thinking about the subject. Did you notice, by the way, how the others just sort of sat back and let you carry the load? How do you suppose we can get them involved? Perhaps, letting someone else kick off the discussion next time?"

The show-off. Some people just have a natural inclination to dominate the discussion. They may be "eager beavers," who sincerely believe that their every experience has to be shared, or true show-offs, who long to impress the instructor and their classmates.

Try asking the show-off thought-provoking questions to slow him or her down. Or you can explain that other students would like to share their opinions too.

The whiner. Sometimes the whiner is a student with a pet peeve. Sometimes the whiner has a legitimate complaint. Most often, whiners are just gripers. Try to get a member of the class to answer the whiner. Or point out that you cannot change policy. If the student persists, indicate you are available to discuss the problem privately.

The rambler. Some people can't seem to pull their thoughts together and go on and on when they speak. It's frequently wise to put up with a reasonable amount of rambling rather than try to discourage the rambler altogether. You can, however, try prodding this person along with a few interjections: "Just a minute—I want to be sure we get all your points down. Your first point was such and such. Now what's your second?"

Another approach is to immediately step in when the rambler pauses. Focus the rambler's attention on the subject matter by restating the relevant points under discussion, and then move on.

The heckler. The heckler is the student who attempts to attack the credibility of the subject or the instructor. In dealing with the heckler, don't allow yourself or the group to get excited. Try to keep tempers firmly in check. You may be able to find merit in some of the points the heckler is making, or get the class to try to. In fact, you can generally count on the rest of the group to help you take care of the heckler. Then move on to something else.

The searcher. In trying to learn as much as they can from you, some students may put you on the spot by soliciting your advice or support of their views. There are times when you must—and should—give a direct answer. However, as a Red Cross instructor, you need to quote Red Cross policy and not personal views. Before you do so, however, try to determine why the information is needed.

The silent type. Newcomers to a group tend to be timid or lacking in self-confidence; many, therefore, simply keep quiet. Other silent types are quiet because they feel superior to the rest of the group. Still others may lack knowledge or interest or feel that they have nothing to contribute.

Get the silent type on an equal footing with the rest of the group by involving him or her in small group discussions. Arouse this person's interest by asking his or her opinion. Find something to compliment sensitive people on the first time they talk, but be sure you are sincere when you do.

Focused on Group Process
To increase the effectiveness and productivity of the class, you need to be aware of group process—how individuals work together in a group to meet the goals of the group and satisfy their own personal needs as well.

Some people are more comfortable in performing a task function that meets the goals of the group. Others, sensitive to individual needs and relationships within the group, prefer the maintenance function.

Task function. Group members tend to be most aware of task-performance and goal-directed activities. The following kinds of actions will directly aid the group to accomplish its goals. You can perform them yourself but encourage and support students' efforts in these directions. The actions include—

- Initiating. Get the group to start working; keep the action going; make suggestions and proposals.
- Informing. Give facts and opinions; point out beliefs and values.
- Seeking information. Ask for facts and ideas.
- Clarifying. Give clear interpretations of information; clarify any statement that may be confusing.
- Regulating. Influence the tempo or redirection of the group's work.
- Summarizing. Pull ideas of the group together so that the group can consider them.
- Testing for consensus. Ask for agreement on a point.
- Evaluating. Help the group evaluate its decisions, goals, and actions.

Maintenance function. As students work together on a task, they interact in a constantly changing network of relationships. Group maintenance refers to those activities that promote the group sense of identity and good working relationships among members. Some of the actions that help build, improve, and maintain working relationships and create an emotional climate conducive to the effective functioning of the group are—

- Expressing feelings. Develop a sense for the feelings of the group members. Help individuals express how they feel in the presence of others.
- Encouraging. Help others by encouraging them, by being responsive and warm, and by recognizing both individual and group accomplishments.
- Compromising. Adjust and settle matters by seeking group consensus. Offer to compromise whenever a conflict of ideas deters a group's activity.
- Standard setting. Suggest standards for the group to achieve.

Focused on Content

This intervention involves ongoing assessment of the learning process. It is a process that involves observing, coaching, and, at times, making changes. From time to time you may need to check on group tasks to determine if they are on target with the intended objective of a task or to monitor the class as a whole to evaluate overall involvement and enthusiasm. In a sense, you are taking the pulse of the group periodically and determining if changes need to be made to facilitate learning. Sometimes it is necessary to repeat information or reteach a part if students are having difficulty.

Focused on Feedback

Feedback, another important intervention, is the ability to correct mistakes in a positive manner by giving students constructive, nonthreatening information about their performance. It is your verbal response to the assessment you make.

There are three types of feedback: negative, positive, and corrective.

- Negative feedback does not promote learning and damages the student's motivation. It is often judgmental and does not give information about what needs to be changed. (For example, "You really did poorly on that skill!") Negative feedback should never be used in teaching.

- Positive feedback is an acknowledgment of a response or action in a nonnegative manner. (For example, "When you talked with your client, you appeared to be well in control of the situation.") It can be a gesture, a nod or smile, or a statement that gives positive reinforcement. Students are often motivated in the learning process by positive feedback. It can be overdone and ineffective if it appears to be insincere or trite.

- Corrective feedback is given by identifying an error and giving the correction. It is particularly useful in the teaching of skills. (For example, "Most of the stroke is being done pretty well. You're having a little trouble with the last part—you're hooking the paddle. Instead, extend the paddle back toward the stern." Another example is, "You seem to be using the correct technique. Do you see any problem with your bandaging? Do you think the dressing will remain in place? How would you fix it?") Corrective feedback is done in a nonjudgmental and positive manner. You often will have to provide the correct answer, but sometimes students can determine the correct techniques on their own, by assessing and stating the results.

In a classroom setting, you should determine if and when it is appropriate to give corrective feedback. In assessing a situation, it may be necessary to talk with students on an individual basis, as you permit them to save face and not be embarrassed in front of the class. But on the other hand, it may be important to provide immediate corrective feedback.

In giving corrective feedback—
- Identify the error or behavior in a nonjudgmental way.
- Define the results.
- Provide or describe the corrective action or lead the student to provide his or her own correction.

Summarizing   In closing a session or segment of a course, the function of summarizing is used to clarify the key learning concepts or objective presented or, in some cases, to test for learning. This action helps to reinforce learning and gives a sense of closure to a segment or topic.

There are many ways to summarize. The instructor may summarize by—
- Reviewing the objectives of the session and discussing key points.
- Asking the class to state what objective was learned.
- Listing key points on newsprint paper or chalkboard.
- Asking key questions.

In summary, to be an effective instructor, you will want to work on developing the characteristics listed for an effective instructor: good communication skills, knowledge of the subject and learning theory, positive attitude, professional appearance, patience and flexibility, and professional behavior. Practicing and getting corrective feedback during training and from your co-instructor when teaching will help you develop these characteristics. Developing instructor characteristics and knowing the correct instructor functions are an important part of conducting a course, which is discussed in the next section.

The mnemonic BASIC—Bridging, Assigning Tasks, Summarizing, Intervening, and Climate Setting—may help you remember the instructor functions.

Unit 4: Conducting a Course

Unit 4: Conducting a Course

In this unit, Conducting a Course, you will learn about the methods used to communicate different kinds of information. The teaching methods for communicating knowledge, attitudes, or skills; the strategy for team teaching (co-instructing); and instructional aids are discussed in this unit.

A teaching method is a way of presenting information for cognitive, affective, and psychomotor learning. To facilitate learning, each teaching method should convey information to the students in a specific manner.

In most Red Cross courses, teaching methods are described in the instructor's guide. However, it is important for you, as a new instructor, to obtain an overall general view of most teaching methods used in Red Cross courses.

Teaching Methods: Knowledge or Attitudes

Red Cross courses demand the use of a variety of teaching methods. Some courses have content that focuses on knowledge of a subject while others try to impart attitudes. In turn, each course can be broken down into lesson plans that may use several teaching methods, depending on what is to be accomplished during that part of the lesson. Methods commonly used in Red Cross courses are as follows:

- Lecturette
- Participative lecturette
- Discussion
- Task groups
- Programmed learning
- Role playing
- Consultation triad
- Simulations
- Brainstorming

Lecturette In Red Cross courses, a brief lecture or instructor presentation is referred to as a lecturette. Lecturettes are used to focus on specific information and to provide a bridge or fill a gap in material given previously.

You should use a number of aids such as a chalkboard, flip chart, or overhead projector to provide students with a visual stimulus along with the spoken word. Possible settings for lecturette include classroom, conference room or lecture hall, and outdoor settings.

Advantages
- Covers a large amount of information to convey facts.
- Can be used with a large group of people.
- Is appropriate to use in groups when an expert needs to present material not readily available to students.

Limitations
- Does not encourage student involvement.
- Works less well for conveying attitudes and application of facts.
- Limits instructor's assessment of students' learning needs.
- Offers no or little opportunity for immediate feedback.
- Allows little opportunity to assess students' understanding.

Tips
The following points are suggested for preparing and delivering a lecturette:

1. Prepare for the presentation.
   - Organize the material carefully and make it concise by developing a main theme and related subtopics.
   - Practice and time the delivery, speaking clearly and modulating your voice so that it is not a monotone.
   - Practice with sound equipment, if needed, for a large group.
   - Arrange the setting so that it is appropriate for the topic. For example, a classroom, the deck of a pool, or the bank of a river may be used.

- Plan how you will stand, sit, or move about in the front of the room (or group, if in a nontraditional classroom setting), trying to remain as close to the students as possible.

2. Provide an overview of the topic first and then introduce the subtopics as they are addressed.

3. Use instructional aids to reinforce points, making sure everyone in the class can see and hear, but not so many aids that their use is distracting.

4. Emphasize key points by repeating them.

5. Use brief examples, when needed, to illustrate important points.

6. Maintain pace, allowing time for students to take notes.

7. Review main points at the end of the lecturette.

8. Leave time and encourage students to ask questions at the end.

9. Plan to follow the presentation with an activity that requires participation to help maintain interest and to facilitate learning.

Since merely sitting and listening is a passive experience, students may not remember much of what was said. Use the four concepts of learning—motivating students, associating information, repeating information, and using many of the senses to make the lecturette more effective.

Participative Lecturette

One similar method used to convey facts is the participative lecturette. It is a short lecture that allows limited student participation through questions that focus on obtaining a specific answer. It differs from discussion, which seeks to involve students' ideas, experiences, and/or knowledge in the learning process.

Advantages
- Provides opportunity to share the learning of some members of the group with all members.
- Tends to focus students' attention from the universal to the particular.
- Can extend to the application of facts.

Limitations

- Encourages only limited student involvement.
- May take more time to present the information than a lecturette.

Tips

The following points are suggested to help prepare and conduct a participative lecturette:

1. Explain the expected outcome(s).

2. Prepare your questions well to obtain specific answers and to avoid excessive discussion.

3. Focus students' attention away from the large, general base of information to a narrower application that is within the students' frame of reference. For example: "Volunteers work in a number of settings within a Red Cross unit including such services as Health and Safety, Disaster, and Military and Social Services. Who can give me an example of the kinds of activities that volunteers would do in each service?"

The participative lecturette, allowing for a more structured response, reinforces a particular point combining the lecture and discussion methods.

Discussion   Discussion is one of the most widely used methods for teaching Red Cross courses. It is a method in which both instructor and participants actively contribute to learning. Possible settings for discussions include classroom, conference room, and outdoor settings that accommodate usually no more than 20 people. It is ideal (but not always possible) for participants to face each other to facilitate discussion.

Advantages

- Allows instructor to clarify values, solve problems, plan action, discuss attitudes, explore related parts of a topic, and work out how to apply what was learned.
- Provides opportunity for an instructor to determine how well students understand the material.
- Builds on previous knowledge.
- Provides a way for students to reach conclusions that consider points of view other than their own.
- Helps students learn to analyze a subject and ask questions.

- Helps students to maintain interest.
- Facilitates remembering since students are analyzing information to draw conclusions.
- Provides opportunity for students to become more involved in the learning situation.

Limitations

- Is time consuming, especially with diverse groups of people.
- Requires a skillful instructor to prevent a few students from dominating the discussion or to keep the discussion on track.
- Is only as good as the combined thinking of the group.

Tips

The following points are suggested for preparing for and holding a discussion:

1. State the topic and time limit, writing it out so that all can see and making sure students understand discussion objective(s).
2. Develop specific questions to meet the objectives of the discussion.
   - Closed questions elicit a yes or no response. For example, "Do you like this?"
   - Open-ended questions stimulate thinking. For example, "What are effective ways to do fund raising?" The use of what, when, where, how, and why questions lead to the generation of more ideas and discussion.
3. Encourage participation.
   - Urge everyone to participate, discouraging domination. This can be done by thanking the person who is dominating for his or her ideas, by asking what others think, or by calling on another person.
   - Encourage students to build on comments of others.
   - Stress that it is everyone's responsibility to make discussion meaningful. Encourage all to participate since they are members of the class. Sharing ideas adds to learning.
4. Reinforce key points or periodically summarize to enhance learning.

5. Keep discussion on track, not allowing students to wander to other topics.

6. Do not let a wrong conclusion go uncorrected, or be embarrassed to say you do not know the answer. Assure students that answers to questions will be found.

7. Turn questions back to the group periodically.

8. Leave time for questions and responses.

9. Be sure to allow participants to do the talking, and listen carefully to what is said.

10. Do not answer your own questions before giving students a chance to respond.

11. Do not get nervous if students are silent for a few seconds. They usually need time to think.

12. Summarize and review what was learned at the end of the discussion.

Task Groups (small groups or buzz groups)

Designs of many Red Cross courses use small groups to solve problems, to focus discussion on answering a question, to look at alternatives, or to develop ideas. Possible settings for task groups may include the classroom, conference room, lecture hall, and outdoor settings. Space should be adequate to work undisturbed and to be comfortable.

Advantages

- Allow students to test ideas more freely.
- Allow students to apply information just learned.
- Encourage group interaction.
- Promote a feeling of equality among group members.
- Promote an environment conducive to interaction by timid students.
- Are more realistic, since this is how most problems are addressed in life.
- Allow students to check for understanding.

Limitations

- Are often time consuming.
- Cause undue pressure for students to respond, in some cases.
- Do not allow for immediate sharing and building of multiple ideas from a large number of participants.

● Do not accommodate groups that work at different rates, making it more difficult to bring task groups back to the larger group.

Tips

The following points are suggested for the preparation and implementation of task groups:

1. Describe clearly the objective and reinforce it in writing.
2. Review or explain any materials used in the task group assignment.
3. Explain the task clearly and post tasks for easy reference, or use a handout.
4. State the time allowed for the task.
5. Ask class to form into groups of three to six (may be done by naming students or by counting off). Instructions may be given either before or after groups are formed.
6. Assign participants or ask for volunteers to report findings back to the entire class.
7. Ask if there are any questions.
8. Circulate among the groups to ensure the learning objectives of the task are being carried out.
9. Give time warning.
10. Reconvene the class for group reports and discussion.
11. Summarize key points and learning objectives that were accomplished.

This method helps to increase individual participation, to build group cohesiveness, and to use creativity in developing solutions or applying concepts to a particular task.

Programmed Learning

Programmed learning uses specially designed teaching materials to guide students through a course, step-by-step, with the instructor serving as facilitator. Most Red Cross programmed courses require the student to use a workbook. Some use audiovisual equipment or computers. Others have a series of stations where a complete skill or parts of a skill are taught.

Programmed learning requires a student to study information and then complete certain tasks or exercises by applying it. Once the task or exercise is completed, the student moves to the next step.

There are two types of programmed learning—self-paced and group-paced. In self-paced programmed learning, each student works alone and sets his or her own pace. In group-paced, students proceed step-by-step through the course as a group.

Advantages (Self-paced)

- Gives all students a common foundation of skills and information.

- Is structured to allow different students to learn at various speeds, in most cases.

- Allows student to work without feeling pressured to keep up.

- Allows students to spend time needed on topics that are most difficult for them.

- Allows fast learners and students already familiar with the subject to move ahead.

Advantages (Group-paced)

- Allows technical skills and information to be taught to a large number of students, using instructors who are not necessarily experts in the subject matter.

- Allows for a pause between steps so students can catch their breath or ask questions before additional information is introduced.

Advantages Common to Both

- Proceeds step-by-step through the course, from less complex to more complex material.

- Encourages remembering by allowing students to answer questions about the material they are learning.

- Brings important new concepts to students' attention.

- Helps students to know immediately whether they understand the material or need additional study to keep them from developing incorrect concepts.

- Lets students participate in and evaluate their own learning.

Limitations of Both Self- and Group-paced Programmed Learning

- Is used only if instructors have specially prepared materials for each student.

- Needs expensively developed materials.

- Does not permit the inclusion of other methods of teaching.
- Does not allow for idea sharing or building.
- Does not usually provide for active interaction with other students.

Tips

The following points are suggested for preparation and presentation of programmed instruction:

1. Make sure students know how they will be taught before the class begins. Students with reading problems can be helped if they have their books before the class begins.

2. At the beginning of the class, make sure each student has all materials.

3. Act as facilitator but allow programmed materials to do the teaching.

4. Familiarize yourself with the programmed material so you can answer questions.

5. Make sure the class area has space available to meet with participants who need to ask questions.

6. Look for students whose attention is wandering, who are working very slowly, or who are frowning or looking confused.

Role Playing   Role playing is the acting out of roles by selected participants. The action is spontaneous; usually there is no script or set dialogue. Participants react to a specific situation and to one another as the role play progresses.

Advantages

- Is used to familiarize participants (students and instructor candidates) with new concepts through experiencing or observing a role.
- Draws out personal feelings and ideas about a topic.
- Allows new skills to be tried, with failure carrying little risk since it is associated with the character portrayed, not the student.
- Is used to act out a situation physically so the students experience the emotions and intellectual decisions involved.
- Teaches empathy, giving students the opportunity to experience how another person may feel in a given situation.

Limitations

- May become a gimmick or entertainment rather than a teaching method.
- Loses effectiveness if students are too self-conscious to play roles.
- Is usually less effective before a large audience because of the effect of large numbers of people on the players.
- Does not allow alternative for players who do not feel comfortable with sharing thoughts and feelings.
- Is often time consuming.

Tips

The following points are suggested for preparing and implementing role play:

1. Introduce role playing and identify the roles.
2. Explain the objective of the role play.
3. Assign participants to roles or ask for volunteers. (Encourage students who like to role play or are not too timid to volunteer.)
4. Brief the players about the situation and their roles.
5. Use prepared materials by giving each player a written description of the character he or she will play or by providing a detailed description of the overall situation, if applicable.
6. Give each player a fictitious name and a sign bearing the role-play name. If the players are to be seated around a table, use name cards.
7. Before the action begins, allow the players time to talk about their roles, but do not let them rehearse.
8. Set the stage by describing the role-play situation to the rest of the class, and introduce the roles and fictitious names of the players.
9. Provide observer sheets or describe to the class particular things for which they should look.
10. Start the role play and let it continue until the interaction slows or the desired information is provided, usually no longer than a few minutes.
11. Ask players and nonplayers to analyze the experience. What happened and why? What were the the motives and feelings

of all involved? What alternatives could there have been to produce the same or better results?

12. Thank the players and debrief them and the group, making a point that the players are now resuming their own identities as they return to the group.

13. Summarize the activities and what was taught.

To vary the role-playing method, stop the action at intervals to solicit the audience's reaction to the situation. Ask members of the audience how they view the players at that point. They may even suggest what the players should say or do next.

Consultation Triad   A consultation triad consists of three students who work together in assigned roles. One student is the consultant, another student describes the "problem," and the third student observes the interaction that occurs between the first two students. The activity involves three rounds; students switch roles until each one has experienced each role. Problems can cover a wide range—from how to handle a disaster victim to what to do in a case of suspected child abuse.

Advantages
- Allows each student to experience receiving help with a problem.
- Allows students to practice giving consultation.
- Gives students experience in observing and evaluating an interaction.
- Has a high degree of student participation.
- Is flexible and an easily prepared teaching method.
- Is easy for students with good verbal skills.
- Provides opportunity for students with less developed verbal skills to participate.

Limitations
- May be time consuming.
- Requires relatively good feedback and consultation skills.
- Needs a large space if there are many teams.

Tips
The following suggestions are offered for the preparation and implementation of a consultation triad:

1. Select a single large room or a series of smaller rooms if privacy is a concern.
2. Divide students into groups of three.
3. Ask triad members to sit so they can hear and see each other well.
4. Provide students with basic guidelines on observing and giving feedback on the subject.
5. Explain the three roles within each group, as follows:
   - One member has a problem and needs help.
   - One member is the helper or consultant.
   - One member is the observer and takes notes on the process but does not engage in dialogue.
   - After each round, the "observer" gives feedback to the "consultant," analyzing how well he or she did.
6. Describe the problem, in general, to the "members to be helped."
7. Give the time frame for the activity (usually 10 to 15 minutes).
8. Allow students a few minutes to think about the exercise.
9. Begin first round by asking "members to be helped" to describe their specific problem or situation to the other two members (the problem may be an actual one).
10. Move from group to group and listen to the dialogue to ensure the triads are focusing on the goal of the exercise; provide corrective feedback, if needed.
11. Repeat the entire exercise a second and third time to give each triad member the chance to play every role.
12. After the third round, reassemble the class to discuss what was learned about the consulting process and about the specific goal of the exercise.

Simulations   Simulation exercises are much like role playing, but no one is assigned to a specific role. Most simulations are written scenarios that imitate lifelike situations in which problems are presented. Members of small groups work together as a team to solve the problem.

Advantages
- Provide for human interaction and understanding that can help students learn from the problems presented.

- Allow students to understand and cope with community and social problems, such as providing disaster relief to an individual.
- Provide, at times, solutions to problems previously thought insolvable by interaction and problem solving.

Limitations

- Are a complex method of teaching and learning.
- Require good communication skills between instructors and students for optimum learning to occur.
- Take a great deal of time.

Tips

The following points are suggested for the preparation and implementation of simulations:

1. Divide students into small groups.
2. Follow the course design, which usually contains the scenario. For example, this could be to plan who should be responsible for coordinating voluntary groups.
3. Coach students to react as if they really were in a position to make the decisions required to do the specific job.
4. Identify the constraints or limitations on the actions.
5. Focus the group's energies on a particular task or concept.
6. Explain that a simulation exercise is a team effort and there is no winning or losing side.
7. Follow with discussion of the points learned from the exercise.

Brainstorming   Brainstorming is a way to attack a problem with ideas, encouraging every possible idea. Creative thinking is more valued than practical thinking. The objective is simply to develop as many new and novel ideas as possible to deal with a problem.

Advantages

- Finds solutions to problems previously thought insolvable.
- Takes a relatively short period of time.
- Rewards freedom of expression and promotes creativity.
- Allows all members of the group to join in.

Limitations

- Limits ideas if phrases such as, "It's against policy," "It won't work," and "We've never done it before" occur.

- Does not meet objectives if ideas are not later refined or ranked.

- Is difficult if the group is unresponsive.

Tips

The following points are suggested for preparation and implementation of brainstorming:

1. Plan for small groups of 8 to 10 or for the involvement of a whole group, if it is not too large.

2. Provide each group access to a chalkboard or another surface on which to write ideas that can be preserved for the discussion later.

3. State as simply as possible the problem to be brainstormed. There should be only one problem to brainstorm.

4. Present the following ground rules:

   - Ideas are wanted in quantity—the more, the better.

   - Criticism is not allowed. All ideas are to be recorded.

   - Freewheeling ideas are welcome. Ideas do not have to be practical or consistent with current policy or procedure.

   - Ideas should be briefly stated.

   - The ideas of others may be combined and improved upon.

   - No individual credit is given. Brainstorming is a team effort.

5. Have each group appoint, if necessary, someone to keep the activity "on track" should anyone start to speak in paragraphs or label other ideas as poor or impractical.

6. Trigger additional ideas with the "else" technique: "Who else, where else, how else, and what else would solve it?"

7. Keep the generation-of-ideas phase going.

8. Reassemble the class (if small groups were used) to sort through the ideas.

9. Select creative ideas, in accord with the goals of the exercise.

10. Find alternative solutions, if that was the purpose of the exercise, and classify into two groups—

    - Ideas that can be tried immediately.

- Ideas that require long-range study, coordination, or large appropriations.

11. Rank the best ideas—decide on the order in terms of what would be most likely to work.

Other Methods Less frequently used teaching methods for transmitting knowledge and/or developing attitudes, including those that do not require instructors, are briefly described below.

Case Study

A case study is usually a written description of a problem and is appropriate for simulating reality or experience, or for evaluating ideas. The advantages are that it requires a great deal of student participation. There are two limitations to the use of case studies: they are difficult to design, and they require considerable time to complete.

Fishbowl

"Fishbowl" describes a seating arrangement in which a large group is arranged into two concentric circles or half circles so that those in the outer circle can observe those in the smaller circle. This arrangement is used to demonstrate skills or group process, but it tends to put those in the fishbowl "on the spot," which is a limitation. On the positive side, fishbowls provide a setup for an exercise. To do it, select participants to role play an established activity structured for observation by those in the outer circle.

Computer-assisted Instruction

Computer-assisted instruction uses the computer as a teaching device and conveys information in an individualized rather than a group setting, allowing students to work at their own pace. Limitations are its expense and the amount of time it takes to develop and test the material.

Satellite Instruction

Satellite instruction is a communication tool in which various methods of teaching can be used. It involves learning through video and/or telephone hookup. Large numbers of participants can be included, but limited numbers can communicate directly. It can be expensive and time consuming to prepare.

Teaching Methods: Motor Skills

Most motor skills require learning some information. You will find, therefore, that a number of Red Cross courses teaching motor skills will have a combination of teaching methods, including some of those just discussed under the methods for teaching knowledge and attitudes.

Skills practice also involves a set of organizational skills to maximize practice and to ensure that students receive corrective feedback. To teach skills you will want to—

- Prepare equipment and the practice area.
- Present an explanation and demonstration (demonstration may be done by video instead of by instructor, as in CPR and Standard First Aid).
- Provide for guided student practice.
- Review skills periodically so that students will remember them.

For most Red Cross courses, the instruction is organized in sequence in the instructor's manual. For some courses, particularly aquatic courses, instructors will have to make certain decisions about how to organize instruction. This will involve deciding how to break down or sequence the skill to expedite student learning. There may be instances in which you need to teach a skill in very small increments; at other times, you may make big leaps. In addition, there may be times when it is best to progressively build skill or come back and reteach parts of a skill on which students need extra help.

Organizing Instruction

The ways to organize instruction to enhance learning of motor skills are—

1. *Part-Whole Approach.* In this approach each part of the skill is presented separately. After all the parts are learned, they are combined and the whole skill is practiced together. For instance, a lifeguard instructor might teach the approach first, then the reverse, then the level-off, then the carry, and finally put them all together and practice the whole skill.

Advantage

- Is appropriate for students who learn best by concentrating on one task at a time.

Limitations

- May hold back students who learn quickly.
- May penalize those students who are not ready to move to the next skill.
- May mean students forget parts learned earlier when they begin to combine parts into the whole skill.

In most instances, the two approaches that follow will be preferable to this approach.

2. *Progressive-Part Approach.* In this approach students are presented a skill and practice by adding on parts to the skill, one at a time, until the entire skill is learned. Examples of this approach occur when teaching students complex skills in swimming and small craft programs. In teaching the crawl stroke, for example, students first learn to do a prone float with kick, then add the arms, and then breathing. When the students can do the part of the skill that was just presented, the next part is added to the sequence of skills. Eventually all parts are added and the entire skill can be practiced and refined.

Advantage

- Provides more room for individual student progress since students practice the previous parts while learning the new parts of the skill.

Limitation

- Allows students time in which to become bored.

3. *Whole-Part-Whole Approach.* In this approach students are presented the whole skill and practice it initially. If a student is having a problem, he or she practices that part separately and then practices the whole skill again. An example of this approach would be teaching the overarm side stroke in an Advanced Swimmer class. The instructor would explain and demonstrate the new skill, emphasizing changes from the stroke (side stroke) they already know. Students then would transfer knowledge and skill from the previously learned skill.

If the instructor thinks the students are having problems with certain parts of the skill, the instructor isolates those parts so that students can learn and practice them.

Advantages

- Is appropriate for simple skills or when students are at an advanced stage and can transfer other related skills.
- Allows students to practice part of a skill separately, then the entire skill.

To teach motor skills to participants, you will provide them with—

- Explanation.
- Demonstration.
- Practice.

Explanation and Demonstration

The explanation and demonstration part of motor skills instruction involves giving a clear definition or description of a skill and showing how it is done. These two activities, explanation and demonstration, can occur one after the other or simultaneously.

Advantages

- Communicate a skill to students quickly.
- Allow for questions and redemonstration of the skill, if appropriate.
- With the video, are done exactly the same each time, promoting a standard of performance.

Limitation

- Do not always allow instructors to know whether students actually understand the demonstration.

Tips

The following points are suggested for implementing explanation and demonstration:

1. Organize and prepare explanation and demonstration prior to instruction.
2. Present the skill first—outside of the medium in which it will be used (e.g., on the pool deck or on a dock, not in the

water or in a boat). Follow with the presentation in the medium in which it will be used (in the water).

3. Make sure that all students can see and hear.

4. Have some students seated or kneeling and others standing so all can see.

5. Ensure that students are not looking into the sun or the glare from the water when conducting a class outdoors.

6. Try to place students so they are not facing something, such as another class, that would distract their attention.

7. Demonstrate skills at the appropriate angle so that the total skill can be easily seen.

8. Follow the skill presentation by slowly demonstrating and explaining the skill for all courses not video driven.

9. Use teaching cues to help students remember the steps, while demonstrating and explaining them or after a video has been shown.

10. Present the skill the way it is to be practiced (e.g., a water safety instructor teaching the prone float would introduce the skill and demonstrate the way it is to be practiced).

11. Repeat the demonstration, except for those courses that are video driven.

12. Follow with a practice session immediately after the explanation and demonstration.

Guided Student Practice

Student practice of motor skills is essential to learning and mastering those skills. Corrective feedback must accompany practice so that students can correct their mistakes and continue to improve skill execution. For aquatic skills, two stages of practice may take place:

1. Out of the water. This first phase reduces the complexity of the practice, allowing the student to go through the movements and receive feedback under close supervision.

2. Supervised practice of the skill in the water.

Advantages

• Provides corrective feedback during the early stages of learning.

• Allows for learning in the medium in which the skill will be performed.

- Involves the learning concept of using the senses—seeing and the kinesthetic sense—in actually doing the skill.
- Uses the learning concept of repetition.

Limitations

- May become boring as students master the skill.
- Requires making certain that students are practicing most of the time. Students who are waiting to practice or who have completed their practice are not learning!

Tips

The following points are suggested for implementing guided student practice:

1. Develop a "photographic eye" that allows you to quickly compare each student's performance against a performance standard.

2. Determine what feedback to provide.

3. Review skills frequently throughout a course, once students have learned a skill.

4. Practice multiple skills task-group style or at stations at the beginning or end of a class. Information specific to each course with skills practice is covered in detail in each instructor specialty course.

The following types of practice show different ways guided student practice can take place.

Drills

Drills are instructor-led practices in which students practice the same skills in unison. Examples of a drill may consist of students positioning the victim in a Standard First Aid course, a group of students swimming a length of a pool, or students sitting on a pier practicing a kayaking stroke. Drills may be—

a. Static Practice

In this type of drill, students stay in place while the instructor moves among them, for example, in a CPR class in which students practice with the manikin or in a Beginner Swimmer class in which students practice the flutter kick while holding on to the side of the pool.

Advantages

- Allows instructor to move around class, assess student practice, and provide corrective feedback.
- Reduces the complexity of the skill for students at the early stages of learning.
- Enables instructor to control pacing of practice.

Limitations

- Allows students time to get bored if drills are not varied.
- Reduces the complexity of the skill: additional learning may not occur when a simpler skill is practiced for a long period.

In aquatic and small craft classes, a static drill usually is followed by a more complex practice.

b. Fluid Practice

This is the type of drill in which students move from one place to another to complete their practice, for example, students in a swimming class practice strokes by swimming laps or students in a canoeing class practice paddling in a straight line across the lake.

Advantages

- Is more like actual execution of the skill.
- Allows students to get considerable practice, if it is organized so little waiting occurs.

Limitations

- May make students spend too much time waiting and not practicing.
- Makes it difficult at times for instructors to provide feedback to students while they are in motion.

c. Wave

This type of drill involves students moving across an area in unison. For example, in an Advanced Beginner Swimmer class, the instructor might have all the students lined up in lanes at one side of the pool. On the instructor's command one person in each lane begins swimming the elementary backstroke and continues until reaching the other side. When the first group is far enough down the pool to ensure that the next group will not bump into them, the instructor has the next "wave" go. This continues until all students have had a chance to practice.

Advantages

- Allows students to practice the skill.
- Allows more practice time, if well organized.

Limitations

- May make students lose too much time waiting for their "wave" to move.
- Makes it more difficult at times for instructor to give feedback while a number of students are practicing at the same time.

There are other drills specific to the types of physical skills taught in Red Cross courses. These will be covered in greater detail in the instructor specialty courses.

Task Practice

Task practice occurs when students are presented a skill and practice it under less supervision than would be used in a drill. Students are assigned a task, told the physical boundaries in which they must practice (e.g., "stay on this side of the room while practicing"), and then asked to practice while the instructor moves about giving feedback. Skill sheets—provided in many Red Cross workbooks—that list the task, the important aspects of the skill, and the associated teaching cues help students remember what to do.

Advantages

- Allows students to devote time to those skills that need attention while also reviewing skills that have been mastered.
- Maximizes student practice time since waiting for directions at each step is not required.
- Allows instructor to move around class, assess students, and provide individual corrective feedback.
- Enables students to develop self-confidence in skill learning.

Limitations

- Needs instructor to develop a task or skill sheet for students, if the course does not provide it.

- Needs instructor to pay attention to students so they do not stop practice to socialize or engage in other activities.

Task practice is a good follow-up to drills when the instructor wants to provide additional practice or review or when students are at a stage where they have learned a similar skill and do not need initial practice under strict supervision.

Station Practice

In station practice, students move from one station to another and practice new skills or add parts to the skills already learned. An instructor or aide may be at each station, or the instructor may supervise a few stations. When an instructor is responsible for more than one station, the instructor assures the students' safety. This can be done by the use of aides or lifeguards. The instructor also needs to make sure students know what to do at each station. (It is helpful to use posters or skill sheets to help students as they move to the new station.) In addition, students need to be practicing skills instead of talking or waiting. Drills or task practice can occur at each station.

Advantages
- Allows students to master the skill before they move on to a more complex skill.
- Allows students to devote time to those skills that need attention while also reviewing skills that have been mastered.
- Enables students to maximize practice time since waiting for directions at each step is not required.
- Allows instructor to move freely about the class to assess students and provide individual corrective feedback.
- Allows students to develop self-confidence in skill learning.
- Allows reduction of the complexity of the skill at the early stages of learning.
- Enables the instructor to control pacing of practice.

Limitations
- May require a number of aides or other instructors.
- May allow students to become bored, practicing the same thing over again.
- Makes it difficult at times for instructor to provide feedback to all students while they are in motion.

Reciprocal Practice

In reciprocal practice, students pair up, one practices the skill, and the other provides feedback, and then roles are switched. It is important that the instructor emphasize those points to which the student must pay particular attention and that students be given examples of how to give feedback to one another.

Advantages

- Allows the practicing student to receive immediate corrective feedback.
- Allows students providing feedback to engage in "mental practice" that helps them to understand the skill better.

Limitations

- Means students may waste time if they do not practice throughout the allotted period.
- Requires skill sheets or posters to assist students giving corrective feedback.

The above methods of teaching for knowledge, attitudes, or skills will assist new instructors in helping students learn. "Practice makes perfect if corrective feedback is given." Using this manual as a reference and applying methods learned in this course will help to improve your instructor skills.

Instructional Aids

Instructional aids, such as flip charts, posters, handouts, manikins, or large equipment (canoes), are used in conjunction with teaching methods to illustrate or demonstrate course content in teaching for knowledge, attitudes, and skills.

As discussed earlier, learning can be substantially increased if students receive information they can see, in addition to the information they hear. Learning also can be increased if students are shown visually how to do something and then allowed to practice the skill. Some things simply cannot be taught with words alone.

Red Cross courses use a variety of instructional aids. A list of recommended instructional aids needed for a course usually is included in the instructor's manual. When the recommendation is specific, no substitutions, such as other films, should be made. When aids are not listed, the instructor may determine what is needed and include this in his or her lesson plan. (The instructor should first check with the Red Cross unit about reserving instructional aids. They should be tested before class.)

If you are not familiar with an instructional aid, practice with it until you are proficient in using it. It is essential to understand how to use instructional aids correctly, since improper use will detract from the effectiveness of the course and your credibility as an instructor. Also be sure that you preview films, slides, and video- or audiocassettes that you will be using.

The following information gives the advantages and disadvantages in using the various kinds of instructional aids. This section also explains how to prepare them (when applicable) and how to use them to improve learning.

Posters, Pictures, and Charts

Posters, pictures, and large charts are used to focus attention on particular information when you want to emphasize it.

Advantages
- Are reusable, portable, and provide for realistic presentation and demonstration.
- Provide visual emphasis of verbal communication.

Limitations
- Are often time consuming and/or costly to prepare.
- Are not always readily adaptable to the teaching environment.
- Are often awkward to carry.
- Are often overused, with instructor becoming too dependent on them.

Tips
The following points are suggested for preparation and presentation of posters, pictures, and charts:
1. Use to clarify ideas.
2. Keep simple in detail and wording.
3. Use large letters, numbers, and pictures that can be easily read from any part of the room.

4. Use a maximum of 10 lines.

5. Use color to highlight key words and ideas.

6. Check for accuracy.

7. Make sturdy so they can be moved without damage.

8. Display only when using. To avoid distractions, cover with blank paper before and after use, if the display cannot be moved or removed.

9. Face the class, not the display, when speaking.

10. Spend time with the display so class has time to absorb the concepts.

Equipment, Models, and Manikins

Equipment, models, and manikins allow for hands-on experience and help students integrate concepts into actual practice.

Advantage

- Provide hands-on experience: e.g., paddling a canoe in a small craft class or simulating a real situation (using a manikin in CPR). For some courses, such as those mentioned, equipment is mandatory to teach the course.

Limitations

- Are often difficult or expensive for local units to obtain.
- Are usually bulky or heavy to move from one location to another.
- Are usually time consuming to set up.

Tips

The following points are suggested for preparation and presentation of equipment, models, and manikins:

1. Be sure equipment, models, and manikins are clean and in working order.

2. Position equipment, models, or manikins so that the entire class can see what the instructor is demonstrating, or so the instructor can see what participants are demonstrating.

3. Maintain eye contact with class members.

4. Encourage hands-on experience, even if it is not required in a course.

Chalkboards   Chalkboards provide another medium to record or display information. They are often readily available in classrooms.

Advantages

- Are inexpensive, flexible, easy to use, and convenient.
- Have a large surface and are erasable and reusable.
- Are often used to communicate topics progressively through outlining.

Limitations

- Are often more time consuming than prepared flip charts.
- Do not allow for saving material to be referred to at a later time.
- Become messy and hard to read.

Tips

The following suggestions are given for preparation of chalkboards:

1. Plan board presentation before class.
2. Use key words or phrases.
3. Draw faint outlines before doing drawings or diagrams. (Be sure you are doing them correctly.)
4. Use white chalk on black and yellow chalk on green boards, if possible.
5. Stand at a 45 degree angle to the board; do not block the view of the class.
6. Fill in one section of the board at a time, always starting at the top and moving down.
7. Keep lines evenly spaced and material in a logical sequence.
8. Print or write in large, heavy letters.
9. Print or draw quickly so student interest will not lag.
10. Face the group when speaking—not the board.
11. Use a pointer, as necessary.
12. Do not play with the chalk.
13. Allow time for students to copy the material.
14. Erase horizontally or vertically (but not both) when finished with materials to eliminate distracting patterns.

Flip Charts (newsprint pads or chart pads)

Flip charts (newsprint pads or chart pads) are used frequently to record student responses or display parts of course content.

Advantages

- Are inexpensive, easy to use, portable, and reusable.
- Are more legible than chalkboards.
- Allow for preparation ahead of time.

Limitations

- Are difficult if material is to be erased or crossed out.
- Have limited writing space.
- Are time consuming if a number of flip charts are to be prepared.

Tips

The following points are suggested for preparation of flip charts:

1. Prepare material in advance, leaving sheets covered until you use them.
2. Use dark (blue, black, purple), broad-tipped marking pens for better visibility and lighter colors for highlighting.
3. Place a sheet underneath to absorb marks if you are not using a water-based marking pen. Also, you may wish to leave a blank sheet to serve as a cover.
4. Use contrasting colors only to highlight key words; otherwise the chart is too busy.
5. Avoid using highly contrasting colors that are difficult to look at.
6. Use a subject heading or title and underline it.
7. Use only key words or phrases.
8. Write only four or five lines per page.
9. Print or write large enough so that the writing can be read from the back of the room; letters should be at least 1 1/2 inches high.
10. Use light pencil lines or a ruled sheet underneath to help write in straight lines (or use preruled paper).

11. Have pieces of masking tape (or other type of tape that will not damage the walls) available to post sheets after removal from easel.

12. Have paper clips or spring clips available to help clip together previously covered material when reviewing sections of content or concepts again.

13. Number each page at the bottom in pencil for easy reference.

14. Place the easel with the flip chart where it can be seen by the entire group.

15. Face the class when speaking, not the flip chart.

16. Allow time for students to copy material (or make a handout of important material).

Overhead Projectors (transparencies)

Overhead projectors are used to show transparencies, drawings, and/or written material to various sizes of groups. The size of the audience depends on whether the transparency can be seen from the back of the room.

Advantages

- Are easy to use in a lighted room and operate from the front of the room while facing the class.

- Are easy to prepare. (Transparencies)

- Are inexpensive, do not take much room to store, and are easily transported. (Transparencies)

Limitations

- Can be boring if overused. (Transparencies)

- Are noisy.

- Have bulbs that burn out and need replacement during the presentation.

- Are difficult to read if handwritten. (Transparencies)

- Are distracting if the transparencies do not cover the projection platform completely.

- Serve as a barrier between the instructor and the class, limiting movement of the instructor.

Tips

The following points are suggested for the preparation and presentation of transparencies:

1. Make transparencies from clean copies or from transparency masters, or use transparency pens on clear acetate. (See Appendix A for instructions on how to make your own transparencies.)

2. Keep the contrast apparent, using black ink or type.

3. Use color to highlight key words.

4. Letters should be at least 1/4 inch high; ordinary typewriter type is too small.

5. Center material on the transparency.

6. Use a subject heading or title.

7. Limit material to only a few lines.

8. Use key words or phrases.

9. Use overlays to show cumulative effect.

10. Place a frame around the transparency for increased ease in handling.

11. Have an extra projection bulb available, and know how to change it.

12. Practice placing transparency on the projection platform so you know it is placed correctly.

13. Place the transparency in the center of the projector before turning on the light.

14. Turn the projector light off before removing the transparency. This eliminates the distraction of materials being dragged across the screen.

15. Use a cover sheet (bond paper or old file folder) to mask information until it is discussed. Uncover one point at a time.

16. Face the class and projector, not the screen.

17. Refer or point to information on the projector—a pen or pencil may be used as pointer.

18. Remove the transparency at the first sign of too much heat (browning, curling, bubbling).

Slides and Slide Projectors

Slides are used to show graphs or other statistical information, as well as pictures and written material.

Advantages

- Are easy to use and store.

- Present dramatic color and pictures to build the presentation and hold interest.
- Emphasize verbal communication through pictures.

Limitations

- Have breakdowns with no backup.
- May make students sleepy or inattentive in darkened room.
- Takes time to prepare slides and may be costly.
- Need a movie screen for good visibility.
- Eliminate eye contact with students.
- Present lighting and visibility difficulties if the room cannot be darkened.

Tips

The following points are suggested for preparation and presentation of slides:

1. Position the slide correctly for insertion into slide tray by—

- Looking through the slide and positioning it so that the picture is oriented correctly up and down and left and right. When you have done this, you will be facing the "back" of the slide.

- Rotating the slide so the top is down, but the front remains facing the screen. Insert the slide into the tray or projector frame.

- Marking the upper right hand corner, once you have determined how the slide should be inserted, so that you or another projectionist will always know how to insert it.

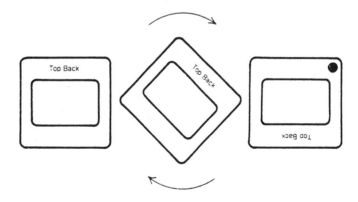

2. Practice the presentation. Work out a "cue" system, i.e., when to change slides.

3. Check cords and have an extra projection bulb available.

4. Present an overview or introduction to the slides while the lights are still on, so the class can see you, and before the projector is turned on so that it does not overheat.

5. Darken room as much as possible while still permitting note taking.

6. Leave a slide on long enough for students to observe key points (15 to 20 seconds or 3 to 4 slides per minute).

7. Use a series of slides in more rapid succession to begin or conclude the presentation, if appropriate.

8. Use 25 to 35 slides (depending on the time period available); showing more slides may become boring.

9. If there is narration between slides, insert slides into every other space and advance to the blank space during the narration, or use a slide-sized piece of cardboard or old slide blacked out with a marker to eliminate the light glare between slides. Newer projectors automatically block the light.

10. Once a slide is off the screen, no longer refer to it.

11. Avoid long "black-outs."

12. When the final slide is shown, turn off lamp but keep the fan on for 5 to 10 minutes to cool the projector.

13. If using audio, taped, or live script, make it concise and to the point. Twenty seconds of commentary per slide is the maximum recommended.

14. After the presentation, follow up with a summary and a conclusion. The summary should include the key points of the entire slide presentation.

Filmstrips and Films

Filmstrips and films are used to convey stories, actions, and other kinds of information.

Advantages

- Present material in a few minutes that would take a lengthy presentation to cover.

- Impart information that could not be presented otherwise.

- Allow students to see movement important for learning certain skills.
- Provide uniform presentation of factual information.

Limitations

- Have breakdowns with no backup.
- May be difficult to find projectors.
- Are expensive to purchase and maintain.
- May make students sleepy or inattentive in a darkened room.
- Eliminate eye contact with students in a darkened room.
- May present lighting and visibility difficulties.

Tips

The following points are suggested for preparation and presentation of filmstrips and films:

1. Consider what teaching goals of the course are and whether up-to-date, accurate, professionally prepared film material is available.
2. Preview the film and review the teaching guide, if one accompanies the film.
3. Have spare projection bulb and exciter lamp (sound projector) available for the projector.
4. Before class, thread the projector and check the operation, completing the following:
   - Thread, following projector directions exactly.
   - Check threading by running projector for one minute.
   - Put screen in place and focus film. Screen should be at least four feet above the floor.
   - Advance film so title and credits are showing.
   - Adjust sound level and tone for clarity.
   - Make sure that audience will be no closer to screen than twice the screen's width and no more than 25 degrees off to each side of the center of the screen.
5. Introduce the film or filmstrip.
6. Guide student learning by listing questions on paper or board or by asking students to look for solutions to particular problems.
7. Warm up projector before turning on lamp.

8. Darken room, adjust sound and focus.

9. As soon as film is over, turn off bulb and turn on room lights.

10. Start discussion immediately. Rewind film at break.

To operate a film projector you should read the directions provided with the projector. If problems arise, refer to the troubleshooting chart and the mock diagram of a projector found in Appendix B.

Videocassettes and Videocassette Recorders (VCRs)

Videocassette recorders are devices used for showing videotapes (videocassettes) on a TV monitor. Generally, the same preparation, such as previewing, is done for both films and videocassettes.

Advantages

- Are often used in a lighted room, but you may have glare on the screen from overhead lights.
- Are easy to stop at points of discussion or skill practice.
- Wear well compared with film.
- Are easy to replay.
- Are less expensive to purchase than 16mm films.

Limitations

- Are expensive. (VCRs)
- Are not easy to secure. (VCRs)

Tips

The following points are suggested for preparation and presentation of videocassettes:

1. Use the counter and note where major segments begin and end.

2. Check all equipment before presentation. Be sure cable connections are compatible and videocassette is compatible with the videocassette recorder.

3. Be sure monitor is large enough for the group to see and is located where everyone can see it.

4. Advance tape so that title is showing when equipment is turned on. (Turn sound off or down when running the initial feeder or ending strip to avoid distractions.)

5. Introduce each segment of the videocassette, if necessary.

6. Replay segments, if needed, for emphasis or review.

7. Summarize key points at the end of the segment or the end of the videocassette.

8. Rewind videocassette at the break or after class.

In general, you should be thoroughly familiar with the aid. Arrange it so that it can be heard or seen by all students. Test it before class to determine if it is functioning correctly. Be sure equipment the students will use is clean and safe. Focus discussion on the students and not on the equipment and cover up visual aids, such as charts, flip charts, and posters until you use them.

In summary, conducting a course involves a number of steps and skills. The teaching process needs to be organized and instructor functions and instructional aids used together to help the students learn and meet the course objectives.

Unit 5: Completing Evaluations, Records, and Reports

Unit 5: Completing Evaluations, Records, and Reports

Evaluation can be defined as determining the significance or worth of something by careful appraisal or study. Ideally, four levels of evaluation occur as a result of teaching: (1) reaction to or feelings about the knowledge and skills obtained; (2) measurement of knowledge or skills through written or performance tests; (3) measurement of changes in behavior by determining how people apply the new knowledge and skills; and (4) determining the impact of the knowledge and skills on an organization or a problem.

As a Red Cross instructor, you will be more concerned with evaluating knowledge, skills, and changes in behavior. You will evaluate before, during, and after a course. The evaluative process usually includes—

- Evaluation, before the course, of students, of self, and of the need for the course.
- Evaluation, during the course, of the students' progress in meeting learning objectives.
- Evaluation, after the course, of the instructional process, of your own performance, and of the students' eligibility for course completion certificates.

Evaluation Before the Course

The evaluation process begins before the course with assessment of course prerequisites and the learning needs of the students. This evaluation step is part of course planning and helps you present the course content at the appropriate educational level, considering the special learning needs of the group. For some Red Cross courses, it may be difficult to do this step because of the difficulty of contacting students before class.

Completion of your own instructor self-assessment form is another evaluation step done before the course begins. This helps you look at the methods or skills on which you would like to work. Further information on evaluation before the course follows in Unit 6, Planning to Teach.

Evaluation During the Course

During the course, students' progress in meeting the learning objectives should be continuously evaluated. Students have a right to accurate evaluation that will aid them in improving their overall performance. Evaluation can be done by observing the students' reactions closely to determine questioning looks, by asking questions of the students to check for understanding, or by observing practice and skill activities. Much of this type of evaluation was covered in Unit 3.

Evaluation at the End of the Course

At the end of a course, students and instructors are requested to complete several types of evaluations. These forms may be used to examine participants' reaction or evaluation of the content, their comfort and confidence with new information, and their evaluation of your performance. You will most likely be requested to complete an instructor reaction sheet for the course and for your teaching performance. Also at the end of the course, you will evaluate the students. Those students who meet the course objectives and criteria for certification will be awarded certificates.

In the long run, the real proof of the effectiveness of a course is not how well students liked it, but how well it prepared them to accomplish the task that brought them to class in the first place. Evaluating such changes can be an expensive and a complex task, but one of which we should not lose sight.

In this section, the criteria for eligibility and for issuing certificates are discussed in general terms.

Criteria for Certification One important function of the Red Cross instructor is to evaluate the student's eligibility for a course completion certificate. Each course has established criteria for eligibility. For some courses, it may be as simple as attending the entire course; in others, a skills test and a minimum score on a written test will be required. Many courses require the following:

- Attendance
- Skills performance
- Passing a written test
- Participation in all activities

Many Red Cross certificates are important requisites for employment or volunteer service in critical areas such as emergency care, public safety positions, and disaster assistance. Therefore, you should make these certification decisions with care. The quality of your certification decisions will affect the quality of many important services provided by the American Red Cross to the American public.

Certificates

For specialty courses, each discipline has a course completion certificate. Additional information, as noted before, will be found in Health and Safety course instructor's manuals; for Disaster Services courses, in *Disaster Training System* (ARC 3065); and in Human Resources and Financial Development course administrative guidelines.

Attendance

Most Red Cross courses require attendance during all sessions. Therefore, the instructor needs to—

- Inform students of the attendance requirement at the beginning of the course to prevent misunderstandings.
- Define the makeup policy, if one exists. For instance, in some courses it may be possible to retake only a section missed, rather than the entire course. In other courses, a student who misses one section may have to make up the entire course.

Some Red Cross courses require a level of class participation for course certification. When you must evaluate participation, some general principles to practice are—

- Defining for students the required level of participation at the beginning of the course.
- Defining any standard of achievement for task assignments.
- Monitoring the progress of each participant through observation and discussion.

- Providing feedback, especially if someone is not meeting the criteria.

Assessing Skills Performance

In some courses, students must pass skills tests. The following general principles are used in assessing skills performance:

- Skills to be performed are listed.
- Instructor and students know the specific outcome intended.
- Instructor knows the standard of performance for each skill.
- The task and standards have been explained to the students.
- The grading system has been explained to the students.

For some specialty courses, skill sheets may be provided on which to check off the successful completion of specific skills. You will learn more about how to judge these skills in your instructor specialty course.

Standard Written Tests

In some of the specialty courses, standard tests are used to determine whether or not a student knows the material or is eligible for a course completion certificate. Specific information about tests will be shared in the instructor specialty courses that include written tests.

Most Red Cross courses that require written tests include published tests and the following instructions in the instructor's manual:

- Required passing score
- Alternative tests
- Retesting procedures

In the few Health and Safety courses in which a test is not provided by the national sector, either the local Red Cross unit should provide a standard test, passing score, and retesting procedures, or the instructor should develop these.

Testing procedures that are to be followed:

- No discussion of specific questions immediately before the test.

- A clear explanation to the students of the passing score and retesting procedures.
- No coaching of participants during the test.
- No substitution, addition, or deletion of a test question without the prior approval of the appropriate Red Cross unit.
- A written test may be administered orally in situations in which a participant has difficulty reading or writing.
- Copies of test questions must be safeguarded to prevent fraudulent use. This means that you should not allow students to take home copies of the test or their answer sheets.
- All completed tests and answer sheets must be turned in to the Red Cross authorizing unit for review by the unit for documentation and verification of test scores.

Records and Reports

Course Record

The *Course Record* (Form 6418) provides information to validate that the course was held. *Course Record* forms help the Red Cross track and measure its instructional efforts. They also are used to monitor instructor activities, to document the certification of students, and to reauthorize instructors. It further documents that course requirements were met and proper procedures were followed in the event legal questions arise.

The purpose of gathering information is to provide the Red Cross with data that will aid it in monitoring the accomplishments of its instructional programs. Information gathered includes data for fund raising and, more importantly, allows the local chapter to verify that an individual completed a particular Red Cross course, which may make the difference in obtaining a job as a lifeguard or as a babysitter.

The *Course Record* forms include information about the certification process, instructional efforts, the number and types of services, the degree of ethnic diversity, and the demand for specific courses. As a general rule, an authorized instructor—one who has successfully completed the Instructor Candidate Training course and the respective specialty course requirements and who is endorsed by a chapter to teach—completes the form after conducting a course for which he or she is authorized.

You will find on this form places for the following:
- Course grade (or pass/fail)
- Student's name, social security number, address, and telephone number
- Student's designation as Red Cross paid or volunteer staff
- Race
- Information on the instructor and co-instructor and any assisting instructors or aides
- Local unit of authorization and address
- Signatures of the instructor and co-instructor, which certify the course was conducted in accordance with the requirements and procedures established by the American Red Cross
- Space for instructor comments regarding the course, supplies, facilities, incompletes, etc.
- Name and address of the Red Cross unit, operations headquarters code, course taught, date course started and ended, the length of the course (in hours), the number enrolled, and number passing or completing the course

The *Course Record* is a four-part NCR form. The original is marked "Red Cross Unit's Copy." Two are undesignated copies that may be sent to other jurisdictions, and the last copy is the instructor's copy.

Participant Reaction Form
You will need to review reaction forms of the participants to evaluate the course. Participant reaction forms are in the course materials or supplied by the service. This information will tell you if the participants liked the course, if the course was administered well, and if the course was what they expected it to be. Most often rating scales are given or open-ended questions are asked to determine satisfaction with the course content and the teaching process.

Questions such as the following are asked:
- Did the course meet your expectations?

- Was the registration process smooth?
- Was the facility comfortable and did it provide a suitable environment for learning?

Questions also are asked about the participants' perception of the effectiveness of the course and the instructor, such as—

- How well do you feel you achieved the following objectives?
- How well did your instructor do the following?
- How effective were the course materials and audiovisuals?

Instructor Reaction Form

The information on the instructor's reaction forms can provide data for recruiting for the course, revising the course, and administering the course. Instructor reaction forms are likewise found in the course materials or provided by the service.

Instructors should consider the following questions when filling out their reaction sheets:

- Were the students adequately prepared?
- Were you satisfied with the support you received from the unit/sponsor?
- Were the learning objectives appropriate to the needs of this group?
- Were students able to meet the stated objectives?
- Did the course go as planned?

Once these questions have been answered, they need to be analyzed and interpreted by the instructor and the Red Cross unit.

Instructor Self-Assessment and Development (Form 5898-J)

As noted above, you will assess how the course went and what kind of a job you did. Your own reactions need to be recorded, and additional information can be obtained from sources such as the reaction forms, written worksheets, and tests. You might want to ask yourself questions similar to the following:

- Were there any points during which students seemed inattentive and disinterested? When? Why?

- Did the students perceive that they were able to meet the course objectives by the conclusion of the course? Were there any trends in the answers? For instance, if 80 percent felt that they could not do the third objective very well, why did this happen? How can you assure it won't happen again?

- How did the students rate you as an instructor? Were there any trends? Can you identify any areas that you might want to improve?

- If the course did not go the way you planned, or you were unable to meet the objectives, are you able to identify what happened? Is the problem with your presentation? What adjustments do you need to make?

- Do you need to adjust your lesson plan, or was it effective for this group?

- If you did not receive adequate support from the Red Cross unit/sponsor, what suggestions could you make to improve the situation?

- Were the students satisfied with the registration process, facility, etc.? Are there any suggestions to improve the process?

- Self-assessment forms can be used on a continuing basis before each course is given and after it is completed to determine areas to develop.

Disposition of Records and Reports

After you review the participant reaction sheets, forward them within 10 days to the appropriate Red Cross unit. For instructor evaluations, follow the instructions on the forms. In some courses, evaluation forms must be sent to the local unit, to operations headquarters, or to national headquarters. You will be given more explicit directions on forms in your instructor specialty course.

In most cases, your *Course Record* forms and reports are turned in as follows:

- For Health and Safety courses, send forms to the Health and Safety director/administrator at your local Red Cross unit.

- For Financial Development courses, send forms to the designated service office in your operations headquarters.

- For Disaster Services, follow instructions in *Disaster Training System* (ARC 3065).

- For Human Resources courses, send the forms to the local Red Cross unit and copies of the Instructor Report and Form 6418 to Training and Instructional Systems Division at national headquarters.

It is recommended that *Course Record* forms for the Instructor Candidate Training course be kept by the Red Cross unit for five years.

In summary, information discussed in this section provides guidance in managing and evaluating a specialty course. Specific information will be provided in each specialty course.

Unit 6: Planning to Teach

Unit 6: Planning to Teach

The components of teaching are planning to teach, conducting, and evaluating a course. Planning is always the first step; but in this course, it is believed that you will have a better idea about what needs to be planned if you first have a good understanding of the meaning of conducting and evaluating. Therefore, the planning unit is presented after the conducting and evaluating units.

Planning is one of the most important ingredients in successful teaching. You will want to consider the following points when you plan to teach:

- Establish an effective working relationship with the Red Cross unit/sponsor.
- Do precourse assessment of participants as individuals and as a group if this information is available in advance, and plan your own development goals.
- Review course materials and objectives.
- Determine time requirements.
- Prepare for team teaching, if applicable, and include time to prepare with your co-instructor.
- Develop a block plan, if needed.
- Select instructional aids, facilities, and equipment.
- Secure supplies and course materials.
- Develop a lesson plan, if one is not provided.
- Set up the teaching area and test equipment.

These points are listed in the order in which it is suggested you carry them out.

Course Sponsor

A Red Cross specialty course may be sponsored locally in chapters, on military stations, at a workplace setting, and in all national sector units as need and resources dictate. Sponsorship refers to the Red Cross unit organizing or offering a course. Course sponsorship is handled in the following ways:

- For Human Resources courses, information is available through the local unit or through the division of Training and Instructional Systems at national headquarters.

- For Disaster Services courses, information may be obtained from Disaster Services at each operations headquarters.

- For Financial Development courses, information is available in each operations headquarters Office of Financial Development.

- For Health and Safety courses, each Red Cross unit offers its own training. Operations headquarters may have current information about selected Health and Safety courses and institutes. Local units with no instructors may negotiate through appropriate management channels to secure instructors from other units.

In most instances, this means that you will be contacted by the sponsor to teach a specialty course at a specific time and location. It is important that you establish and maintain a good working relationship with the sponsor. Some Red Cross units do more planning than others, and you need to be clear about what is expected of you and what the unit will do.

Assessment

Participants in Red Cross courses fall into several groups. One group includes external audiences, who are, in general, from "outside" the Red Cross—interested citizens, businesses, schools, organizations, and agencies. Another group is internal and consists of Red Cross paid and/or volunteer staff. In either case, if possible, you should assess the individual learning needs of the participants to determine what skills, knowledge, and experience they bring to the class collectively. This information helps in planning so that participants are challenged but do not have difficulty learning. Other factors are individual physical impairments, learning preferences, and education level.

It is helpful to know why the participant is taking the course. Is it a job requirement? Is it for self-development? Or is it for another reason? You also will want to determine if participants have met all course prerequisites.

Information can be gathered from preregistration forms, from Red Cross unit files, from application forms, and from the participants themselves.

Plan for Personal Development Goals

Instructor Self-Assessment and Development (Form 5898-J), found in Appendix C, is designed to help you assess your competencies in teaching skills. Complete the form before a teaching assignment to give you a picture of your strengths and the areas you want to develop. When team teaching, you should use the self-assessment form when you plan with your co-instructor.

The following information suggests the process for using the form:

- After completing the *Instructor Self-Assessment and Development* form, identify several skills you wish to develop or learning goals you wish to achieve.
- Use the back of this form to record areas you wish to improve and how you plan to improve them.
- Under the first column, headed "Objectives," list the areas you wish to improve or other self-development goals.
- In the second column, headed "Plan for Accomplishing," write the steps that you will take to meet your goals.
- In the third column, "Resources," list any resources that you will need to meet your goals.
- An example for each heading is given on the next page.
- Enlist the support of your co-instructor (if you have one) in your development plan.

Objectives	Plan for Accomplishing	Resources
Managing time	Determine length of time for each section of material.	Instructor's manual
	Review block plan.	Block plan
	Review lesson plan for organization of content.	Lesson plan
	Determine beginning and ending time.	Clock
	Have co-instructor give time cue, e.g., "five more minutes."	Co-instructor

Course Objectives

Thoroughly review the course objectives. "Walk through" the course by reviewing the instructor's manual and participant's materials (workbooks, handouts, or attachments) to see how the course objectives are met through the various teaching methods, activities, or practice sessions. Observe how the course "progresses" from one topic or skill to the next. Note the audiovisuals to be used and how they enhance the objectives. This review with help refresh your memory on the key points of the course.

Time Requirements

Note time requirements for your specialty course. Some courses have optional times for teaching, such as one day (eight hours of instruction), or two days of four hours of instruction. Some courses do not have options, and the time cannot be altered. Other factors to be concerned with when considering time are—

- Your availability as instructor.
- Availability of facility(ies) and equipment.
- Availability of a particular group of students.
- Time required for breaks.
- Times for beginning and ending.
- Lead time for ordering materials and equipment.

Team Teaching

When you team teach, there are two roles—lead and support. You will decide together which one will assume the lead for a particular portion of the content. The responsibility of the supporting role includes providing logistical support, assessing the group, assisting during the instruction, and taking cues when your co-instructor is the lead instructor. Assistance includes either physically assisting with the instructional aids or providing clarification and adding to the content to make a point. Throughout the course, you will make several transitions from being lead instructor to being support instructor.

Team teaching—

- Allows one team member to make a presentation while the other sets up materials, writes on the chalkboard, serves as a resource, and helps to "read the group."

- Allows co-instructors to share and learn from each other, complementing each other's teaching styles.

- Lightens the load of teaching.

- Exposes students to two role models and different areas of expertise.

- Allows the class to be larger in many instances.

- Allows less experienced instructor to focus on areas to build teaching skills.

- Provides assurance of a backup if one instructor has an emergency or is ill.

If you co-instruct regularly, remember to change the sections in which you are the leader in order to maintain and improve your ability to teach the whole course. Students generally enjoy and respond to the constructive contrast of team teaching—different voices, styles, and approaches. The effectiveness of the course depends on the combined efforts of both instructors.

Block Plan

A block plan is an outline of the course times, objectives, and content for each session. Developing a block plan helps you organize your material or course content within a time frame. Furthermore, it helps you identify what is needed for each session.

In some training courses, block plans are developed for you. A sample is shown in Appendix D. Once the block plan is complete, you will know what is needed on a given day, and you can make arrangements to secure it.

Instructional Aids, Facilities, and Equipment

You may be called on to select the facility, unless this has already been done by the sponsoring or host unit. Factors to consider in selecting the facility include—

- Number of students expected.
- Types of activity during the course.
- Cost of the facility.
- Space needed for teaching methods and equipment required for the course.
- Location.

You may also need to secure or order equipment and special instructional aids, such as manikins or a VCR. Confer with the host unit to determine the availability of required aids and equipment.

Supplies and Course Materials

Specialty course instructor's manuals often list the supplies needed for the specialty course. These may include the following:

- Name tents
- Name tags
- Magic markers
- Newsprint pads
- Masking tape
- Chalk and erasers
- Pencils
- Writing paper

Determine what course materials are needed. These may include the following:

- Transparency masters
- Workbooks
- Textbooks

- Handouts
- Attachments
- Tests
- Evaluation forms
- Videocassettes
- Slides
- Films
- Posters

In some instances, you will need to order course supplies and materials. In others, the sponsoring unit will secure them for you. And in still other instances, operations or national headquarters will send the supplies and course materials to the unit where you will be teaching. These details will be explained in your instructor specialty course. It is the instructor's responsibility to determine what needs to be done to ensure that all materials and equipment are available.

Lesson Plans

Most Red Cross courses already have lesson plans. In those courses that do not have lesson plans, you will need to develop them. Samples are found in Appendix E. Although lesson plan formats may vary, most lesson plans contain the following elements:

- Objectives
- Material to be covered
- Outline of the content
- Teaching methods and learning activities
- Cues or key words
- Plans for providing feedback
- Bridges or transitions between activities
- Time allocations
- Announcements to be made before or after class

Different courses may emphasize different elements. If you are teaching a course in which a demonstration and a skill will take place, you will need to include a lesson plan that outlines the demonstration.

Classroom Setup

The physical arrangement of the classroom or teaching area affects the way students learn. Always take time before class to make certain that everything is in order.

- Check lighting, ventilation, and temperature, as learning is hindered in a room that is stuffy or poorly lit or too hot or too cold.

- Arrange the room so that you are able to get close enough to students to make eye contact.

- Place visual aids so all students can see them. Set up all equipment prior to the start of the class and test it, checking sound for volume and visuals for clarity. Don't forget extra projection bulbs.

- If holding a class outdoors, make certain you are able to keep your back to the wind and your students' backs to the sun.

- When needed, determine where group practice or task groups will take place and how to move the students.

(When you conduct a class, post Red Cross identification signs in a conspicuous place to help students find the classroom. The local unit can provide posters and paper flags for this purpose. Also post a placard that identifies you as the course instructor.)

Certain seating arrangements facilitate interaction between you and your students and among the students themselves. The arrangement is dictated by the teaching method.

- A lecture or slide presentation lends itself to the theater style of seating in which students face the lecturer or the presentation as they would the actors in a play.

- The U-shaped and closed-circle styles of seating are more effective when you want more interaction, for example, when you are leading discussions.

You can set up tables, chairs, and desks indoors or outdoors—on a grassy spot or a pool deck. When convenient, students can even sit on the grass. Making the best physical arrangements does not ensure flawless interaction in the classroom, but it goes a long way toward ensuring student attention and promoting successful communication.

Illustrations of some common seating arrangements follow:

Suggested Room Arrangement With Single Large Table

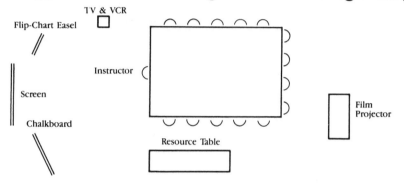

Suggested Room Arrangement With Small Tables

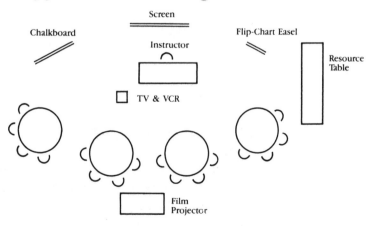

Suggested Room Arrangement
in a Square

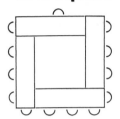

Suggested Room Arrangement
in a Herringbone

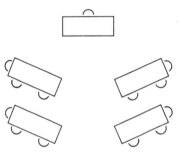

Suggested Room Arrangement
in a "U" Shape

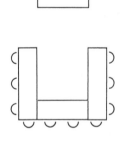

In summary, planning the course is the first step in the instructor responsibilities of planning to teach, conducting, and evaluating a course. Planning for a course requires a number of steps that involve the local unit, your co-instructor, and information about participants. In addition, block plans and lesson plans help you to plan what is needed to conduct the course. Your personal and professional goals should also be considered during the planning process.

Unit 7: Representing the Red Cross

Unit 7: Representing the Red Cross

The previous sections focus on information to help instructor candidates become effective instructors. This section emphasizes being an effective representative of the American Red Cross and describes the importance of teaching in the Red Cross.

The Importance of Being a Red Cross Representative

For those of you who will be teaching primarily to community groups, YOU are the Red Cross, as you may be the only representative with whom citizens come in contact. This section presents you with information about the Red Cross to help you be an ambassador and a role model as you teach courses for the American Red Cross.

A video, entitled "Behind the Headlines," highlights the history of the American Red Cross and the services and programs it offers today. Additional information can be found in Red Cross books and pamphlets and in your instructor specialty course. An example of one pamphlet that is a good reference is *The American Red Cross: A History of Helping Others* (ARC 4627) and its companion brochure, *People Helping People* (ARC 4628). Also, you may ask your Red Cross authorizing unit to assist you in learning more about Red Cross history.

The Importance of Training Within the Red Cross

Training has an important role in the Red Cross, as paid and volunteer staff learn how to deliver effectively vital services that have consequences nationally and worldwide. Uniform training is especially important in Disaster Services and Health and Safety. Ensuring uniform and consistent response to disaster victims is a major task. Consistency of information and skills are needed nationwide because disaster workers most likely will be teamed with others who were trained at different Red Cross sites. Since the American Red Cross is mandated by its congressional charter to provide disaster services, it is imperative that instructor candidates realize the importance of their responsibility to teach the correct policies and procedures.

Also, this responsibility is just as important in Health and Safety, where correct and consistent information may mean the difference between life and death. It is very important that accurate techniques be demonstrated according to the course lesson plans, that course objectives be met, and that the integrity of the course design be maintained. Not following the course design could have legal implications as well.

Human Resources and the operations headquarters Offices of Financial Development offer staff development courses, which are important in providing the best and most effective support to mandated services and the other disciplines.

Just as it is important to understand training in the Red Cross and recognize the significance of its mission and history, it is equally important for instructors to practice the organizational ethics found in the Five Key Commitments.

Five Key Commitments

The Five Key Commitments, developed by Keilty, Goldsmith, and Boone, were adapted for American Red Cross paid and volunteer staff. Awareness of these commitments helps you be more effective in providing service or information to the public or to Red Cross paid and volunteer staff. Information found in Appendix F will help you understand the following text.

No matter what your affiliation is with the Red Cross, as paid or volunteer staff, your actions should reflect the Five Key Commitments.

Commitment is described as (1) commitment to the *organization*, to help build and support it and its management; (2) commitment to *customers*—those individuals whom we serve or teach, both internal and external to the organization; (3) commitment to the *task* or mission, to keep the right focus, to be action oriented, to break work into achievable components, and to be committed to excellence in the achievement of that task; (4) commitment to the *people*—individuals with whom you come in contact and the team with whom you work—to allow them to use innovative ideas and to show them positive concern and recognition for what they accomplish; and (5) commitment to *yourself* as a "manager" of tasks, acting on constructive advice to learn and grow and to develop your own talents.

These elements describe the commitments expected of paid and volunteer staff as they execute their responsibilities as Red Cross instructors.

Ethics

Ethics is an important part of your commitment to the Red Cross. As part of the American Red Cross, each of us is responsible for and committed to fulfilling the Red Cross mission by improving the quality of human life; enhancing self-reliance and concern for others; and helping people avoid, prepare for, and cope with emergencies. To carry out activities in support of these commitments, we find it necessary to observe the "fundamental standards of our culture: telling the truth, keeping promises, respecting individuals, being fair. Each of us is responsible for maintaining the highest standards of ethics at the American Red Cross." These statements are found in *Ethics: Our Commitment at the American Red Cross* (ARC 9004).

Instructor Agreement

The *Instructor Agreement for American Red Cross Instructional Courses* (Form 6574) has been developed for instructors. It states that as a Red Cross instructor you will recognize that you are a member of a select group that must maintain high standards, that you are responsible for teaching the information and skills considered vital by the Red Cross, and that you will impart knowledge and skills in a professional manner. You will also complete all training required to achieve and maintain certification as a Red Cross instructor. In addition, you will teach Red Cross courses only when you have been authorized by the Red Cross chapter or unit in whose jurisdiction you will serve. More information on the instructor agreement will be given to you as you progress through the steps to becoming an authorized Red Cross instructor.

In summary, being a good Red Cross representative and role model involves demonstrating your effectiveness by—

- Applying the information about the learning process.
- Knowing how to conduct an effective course by understanding how to use the appropriate teaching methods and skills.
- Being personally effective as a good communicator and professional in your conduct.
- Executing the evaluation process for the participant and for yourself, the instructor.
- Doing what is expected as an instructor in planning for the course and the necessary follow-up.
- Sharing the importance of Red Cross history and its mission, carrying out the Five Key Commitments, and representing the American Red Cross.

You will have the opportunity to apply the knowledge you obtained in the instructor candidate course to the specialty instructor course. This information provides you with the foundation to build on as you move on to the next step of instructor candidate training.

As you learn more about the American Red Cross, you will discover many more opportunities for volunteer leadership, such as serving as instructor trainers, as committee chairmen, on local boards of directors, and as service chairmen. You have many opportunities and rewards ahead of you as you begin your Red Cross adventure.

Glossary

Affective Domain A learning domain that includes attitudes that influence feelings or emotions and affect behavior.

American Red Cross Mission Statement "The mission of the American Red Cross is to improve the quality of human life, to enhance self-reliance and concern for others, and to help people avoid, prepare for, and cope with emergencies. It does this through services that are governed and directed by volunteers and that are consistent with its congressional charter and the principles of the International Red Cross." Adopted by the Board of Governors, February 12, 1984.

Area Offices American Red Cross offices in Stuttgart, Germany (European Area Headquarters), and Camp Zama, Japan (Far East Area Headquarters).

Assigning Tasks An instructor function performed when students are asked to do a task, such as an exercise or case study.

Authorized Acceptance according to national authorization guidelines by a Red Cross unit to teach a Red Cross course in that unit's jurisdiction.

Authorizing Unit The Red Cross unit that has the authority to authorize instructors to teach. The authorizing unit may be the local unit or the national sector, depending on the service and the level of the course.

BASIC Mnemonic that stands for instructor functions of bridging, assigning tasks, summarizing, intervening, and climate setting.

Block Plan An outline of the available time, the objectives, and the content for each class session.

Body Language Nonverbal communication expressed through gestures, facial expressions, posture, or gross body movements.

Brainstorming   A teaching method in which a problem is approached or ideas generated by a group. All possible ideas and creative thinking are encouraged.

Bridging   An instructor function that uses descriptive words to link ideas or one section of a course to the next to provide the continuity necessary for learners to have a connected learning experience. It supports learning by association.

Certificate   A document formally recognizing that an individual has successfully completed the minimum requirements of a Red Cross course of record.

Certified   Receipt of a completion certificate when a participant has met all minimum course requirements of a Red Cross course.

Climate Setting   An instructor function that provides an environment in which effective learning can take place from the beginning of the course to the end.

Cognitive Domain   A learning domain that relates to knowledge, facts, concepts, and application skills, also a process of knowing—being able to reduce information to factual knowledge.

Communication   An exchange of information that involves a message, a sender, and a receiver.

Consultation Triad   A group of three participants working together in the assigned roles of the helper; the participant, who receives help; and the observer, who provides feedback.

Corrective Feedback   Feedback that is nonjudgmental and nonthreatening, identifies the error, defines the results, and provides the correct information in a positive and supportive manner.

Co-teach   Sharing full or 100 percent participation in course leadership with one or more instructors. Also known as team teaching.

Course Leadership   Full or 100 percent participation by an instructor/instructor trainer in the planning, teaching, reporting, and evaluation of a course.

Course Objective	A statement of intent describing a proposed change in skills, knowledge, or attitudes of a learner after completing a learning experience.
Course of Record	A course taught, properly reported, and accepted by a Red Cross unit.
Course Record (Form 6418)	A form completed by ICT instructor trainer and instructors of other courses and turned in within 10 days after course completion to the Red Cross unit in whose jurisdiction the course was taught. This record is used to document certificate issuance, instructor teaching activity, course grades (when required), and service activity for statistical reports. It may be used as a legal document.
Course Record (Form 6418-A)	A continuation of Form 6418 that has space to list required participant information. It should be used when there are more participants than can be listed on the *Course Record* (Form 6418).
Cross Training	Receiving certification and authorization in another discipline or service or within a discipline or service by meeting instructor specialty course prerequisites, getting approval from the authorizing unit, and successfully completing other requirements such as the instructor specialty course.
Discussion	A teaching method in which an instructor announces a time frame and a topic during which participants are encouraged to talk about the topic, to interact, and to build on each other's ideas. Key points are usually summarized at the end.
Domain	An area of related activities defined in language where observations, distinctions, assessments, and evaluations of competency are made. For example, the cognitive domain contains awareness, judgment, and factual information.
Drills	Repeated exercise(s) or practice of a skill.
Enrolled	Currently assigned to a class and paid/formally committed to it.
Explanation, Demonstration, and Practice	A method for teaching motor skills in which the skill is explained, shown to the participants, and then practiced by the participants.

Extended Authorization	Permission granted to a local Red Cross instructor from another jurisdiction to teach within a unit's jurisdiction.
Facilitate	In teaching, to make understanding easier and clearer, for example, by promoting discussion or asking leading questions to enhance learning.
Fail	A course grade signifying that a participant has not passed ALL the required skills and/or a written test and prefers not to be retested, or does not pass a retest.
Feedback	Information about the value or efficacy of a course, program, service, project, or behavior, which is received by students, interviewees, instructors, or others.
Five Key Commitments	Commitment to self, commitment to the organization (American Red Cross), commitment to customers (students), commitment to people (course sponsor or co-instructor), and commitment to the task (helping students learn). Adapted from Keilty, Goldsmith, and Boone.
Graphic	A visual presentation that illustrates an idea using a picture or chart.
Guided Student Practice	Supervised practice in which a student is engaged.
Host Unit	The unit responsible for providing an appropriate site, providing necessary logistics, and supporting the training activity in cooperation with the sponsoring unit.
Incomplete	A course grade signifying that a participant is unable to complete the course because of certain circumstances, such as illness or a death in the family. An incomplete is given only when arrangements to complete the training have been made.
Instructor	A member of a select group of individuals authorized to serve as agents of the Red Cross by teaching designated American Red Cross basic courses within a unit's jurisdiction and imparting knowledge and skills consistent with American Red Cross policies, procedures, standards, and guidelines.

Instructor Agreement (Form 6574)	A form signed by Red Cross instructors as required by the service before teaching a Red Cross course. It explains the rights and responsibilities of both the instructor and the Red Cross unit of authorization.
Instructor Candidate	The term used to describe a person from the time of acceptance into an instructor training course until successful completion of an instructor specialty course and authorization as an instructor.
Instructor Specialty Course	A course that prepares instructors to teach a specific course, for example, CPR, Emergency Assistance to Families, or Career Directions.
Instructor Trainer (IT)	A member of a select group of individuals who exemplify the qualities of the American Red Cross and serve as role models for instructors and other instructor trainers. ITs serve as agents of the Red Cross and are authorized by a Red Cross unit to teach Red Cross instructor courses such as ICT and specialty courses for some services. An IT may assist the authorizing unit with training updates, recruitment, or other leadership responsibilities.
Intervening	An instructor function that clarifies, modifies, or directs content or group process during the class for the purpose of facilitating the outcomes of the learning process.
Kinesthetic Sense	A sensory experience, stimulated by bodily movement, that helps you know how and where your body is moving.
Learning	A process of change through which people acquire new knowledge, skills, or attitudes as a result of some type of study or experience.
Learning Style	A term used to define students' learning preferences or orientations at four levels: personality, information processing, social interaction, and instructional methods. This information helps instructors to be more sensitive to the differences that students bring to the classroom.
Lecturette	A teaching method in which the instructor gives a brief lecture or presentation, focusing on specific information that helps to provide a bridge or fill a gap in material given previously.

Lesson Plan	An outline for teaching a lesson or class that usually contains objectives, an outline of content, teaching methods, learning activities, cues or key words, plans for providing feedback, etc.
Minimum Enrollment	The least number of students that may be enrolled for a class to be designated as a course of record. Different courses have different minimum numbers.
Mnemonic	A device or code used to assist the memory.
Motivation	An inward impulse or drive that causes one to act; an incentive.
Motor Skills	Skills that include use of muscular motion as well as information. Also referred to as psychomotor skills.
National Headquarters	The principal office of the American Red Cross, located in Washington, D.C.
National Sector	A term meaning the national headquarters, operations headquarters, Services to Armed Forces field stations, and all other organizational units, except chapters and Blood Services regions.
Objective	A description of standards that participants are to meet by the end of instruction.
Operations Headquarters	The principal American Red Cross office of the administrative jurisdiction in which chapters and Blood Services regions are located. These offices are located in Burlingame, California (Western Operations Headquarters); St. Louis, Missouri (Midwestern Operations Headquarters); and Alexandria, Virginia (Eastern Operations Headquarters).
Part-Whole Approach	A way of teaching and practicing a physical skill that focuses first on one part of a skill at a time and then on all the parts together.
Pass	A course grade signifying that a participant has successfully completed ALL required skills and written tests according to national standards.

Prerequisite Training	Training, defined in a course instructor manual or instructor trainer guide; in program administrative guidelines; or in course fact sheets, that must be completed by course participants prior to the first session of the course.
Prerequisites	Criteria, defined in a specific course instructor manual or instructor trainer guide, or in program administrative guidelines, that must be met by course participants prior to the first session of the course.
Programmed Learning	A teaching method that uses teaching materials to guide students through a learning experience, step-by-step, with the instructor serving as facilitator. It can be self- or group-paced.
Progressive-Part Approach	Breaking knowledge or skills into small components and progressively adding on parts of the skill until the entire skill is learned.
Reauthorize	The act of becoming authorized again by meeting all national requirements.
Record Card	A card maintained by the authorizing unit on instructors/instructor trainers that contains general demographic information, Red Cross teaching history, and current authorizations. May be maintained manually or on a computer.
Red Cross Unit	A Red Cross chapter, a military station, a field service territory, an operations headquarters, or national headquarters.
Role Play	The acting out of roles by selected students or by the instructor(s) in which they react spontaneously to a situation or to each other. Role play also can be scripted.
Skill	Cognition or psychomotor ability to perform a task or activity.
Specialty Course	The specific course(s) that the instructor candidate prepares to teach.
Sponsoring Unit	The unit that makes arrangements to conduct and manage a course.
Task Assignment	Procedure for individual or group learning activities.

Transfer of Authorization Term used to describe a Red Cross unit's acceptance of a current instructor/instructor trainer from another Red Cross unit to teach within the accepting unit's jurisdiction on a permanent basis.

Unit Manager A person responsible for the overall management and oversight of a Red Cross unit, e.g., chapter manager, station manager, field service manager.

Value–Laden Statement Statement in which values are expressed that represent something a person prizes or cherishes.

Volunteer An individual who, beyond the confines of paid employment and normal responsibilities, contributes time and service to assist the American Red Cross in the accomplishment of its mission.

Whole–Part–Whole Approach An entire concept or skill is presented, then specific parts are explained through added explanation/demonstration, followed by guided practice, then combined again into the whole concept or skill.

Withdrawal of Authorization Removal of an instructor/instructor trainer authorization for due cause.

Appendixes

How to Make Transparencies

Special acetate sheets are available to duplicate transparencies from a master copy for use with an overhead projector. There are different types of acetate sheets made for specific copying machines. Make certain that you have the correct type for your copy machine. Clear or colored sheets of acetate are available. The copying process is as easy as making any copy on a photocopy machine, and many manufacturers also include directions for making transparencies. In general, follow these steps:

1. If making more than one transparency, fan the sheets of acetate to allow them to feed easily.

2. Place the sheets of acetate on top of the paper in the feed tray, making sure that the opaque strip is at the feeding (leading) edge of the tray.

3. Place the original (transparency master) on the document glass and produce a single transparency to make sure it is what you want.

4. Set the copier's quantity selector to the appropriate number of transparencies and press the start button, if additional copies are desired.

5. Remove any unused sheets of acetate from the feed tray after the run is completed.

6. Place the transparency on a cardboard frame (which can be purchased commercially) and put masking tape at each corner of the transparency on the back. The frame allows for ease in handling and helps protect the edges of the transparency but is not required for use.

7. If the transparency is not numbered, write on the frame the order in which it will be used.

Troubleshooting Projectors

Becoming a Good Projectionist

With practice, almost anyone can become a good projectionist. Some of the same considerations that apply to making a slide presentation also apply to projecting a film. As usual, the key to a trouble-free presentation is advance preparation, including, if needed, practice in using the equipment.

Before the class meets, arrange the best possible viewing conditions. The first considerations are the physical environment, including some things we tend to take for granted, such as a room large enough to seat the class that is adequately ventilated and that can be darkened sufficiently. Locate light switches and electrical outlets. Find an extension cord, if one is needed, and have a supply of extra bulbs on hand in case one should burn out.

Situate the screen so that it is not too close to the audience. A good guide is to have the chairs no closer than twice the width of the screen and no more than 25 degrees off to either side of the screen's center.

Provide a firm, level stand for the projector; be sure it is high enough to prevent or reduce the picture distortion that takes place if the projector is substantially lower than the screen. Position the projector so that, when the film is projected, the picture is centered on the screen and fills the screen as completely as possible. If centering is not possible, the picture frame should be parallel with the edges of the screen. When a separate speaker is used, it should be placed near the screen and off the floor.

Focus the picture and then, if you're using sound, check the volume from several places in the room. When the sound level seems about right, raise the volume slightly to compensate for the difference in sound when an audience is present.

How to Troubleshoot Overhead Projectors, Slide Projectors, and Filmstrips

Troubleshooting is simple. If the projector is not functioning at all or no image is being projected, the projector is not receiving electrical power or the lamp is burned out. Check out the system in the following order:

1. Check for power.
2. Check that the projector is switched on.
3. Check for a defective projection bulb.
4. Check for proper placement of the transparency or slide tray on the projector.
5. Check for proper placement or insertion of the remote control plug.
6. Clean the lens.
7. Focus properly.

How a Movie Projector Works

Sixteen-millimeter film has sprocket holes on one side and the sound track on the other. (See sketch below.) To lead a reel of 16mm film onto a projector, position the reel so that the sprocket holes are on the side of the film closer to you and the sound track is closer to the projector.

The path of the film is shown in the diagram on the next page. Sprockets 1 and 2 feed the film uniformly through the gate, where the projection bulb shines through the film and produces the image on the screen. The image is focused through the lens.

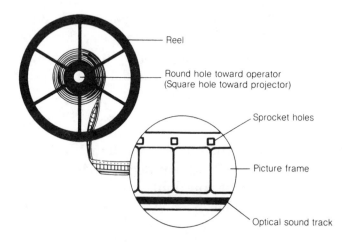

Reel

Round hole toward operator (Square hole toward projector)

Sprocket holes

Picture frame

Optical sound track

The loops are necessary to provide sufficient flexibility to the film so that one picture frame at a time can be stopped in the gate momentarily. From sprocket 2, the film passes around the sound drum, which keeps the film a precise distance from the photosensor. The photosensor is activated by the exciter lamp that shines at varying intensities through the film's sound track. The tension rollers are designed to keep the film tightly secured around the sound drum. From there, the film passes around sprocket 3 to the take-up reel.

The principle is the same for 8mm projectors with sound, although there is no optical sound track (it is magnetic).

Not every 16mm or 8mm projector is exactly like the diagram, but this explanation and the diagram apply to most projectors. Instructors should also check the directions provided with the projector they are using.

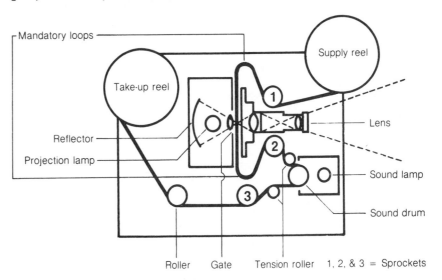

How to Troubleshoot a Motion Picture Projector

The following troubleshooting chart is a compilation of many manufacturers' recommendations. You should also read and refer to the instruction booklet provided by the manufacturer. The booklet will undoubtedly contain some special troubleshooting hints for the projector you are using.

TROUBLESHOOTING

Problem	Possible Causes → Speaker cable	Amplifier off	Exciter lamp defective	Film path dirty (Gate or sound)	Film improperly threaded	Projection lamp defective	Lamps not properly seated in socket	Volume control defective—off-too high	Defective fuse	Dirty lens	Silent/Sound switch improperly set	Dirty film	Power cord defective or not plugged in	Lost film loop
Projector runs but no sound	X	X	X	X	X	X	X							
Distorted Sound	X			X	X	X	X				X	X		
Projector runs but no picture				X	X	X								
Distorted Picture				X	X					X		X		X
Partial Picture				X						X		X		
Alien noises from speaker or projector	X		X	X			X				X	X		X
Picture, sound not synchronized				X										
Picture jumps erratically				X										
Projector fails to operate									X				X	
Picture is series of continuous frames				X	X									X

120

American Red Cross

Instructors: Using the assessment categories (A, B, C, and D) described below, rate yourself as well as you can on each of the following instruction skills.

> A—Little or no experience in this
> B—Some experience but uncertain degree of skill
> C—Some skill
> D—Good skill

A	B	C	D	INSTRUCTION SKILLS
				1. Planning and managing physical environment (tables, seating, lighting, audiovisual aids, papers, etc.)
				2. Setting the climate with a new group, understanding how members of a new group, including myself, feel about participating and being included; maintaining an effective learning climate
				3. Interpreting, applying, and presenting theory
				4. Assigning tasks and giving instructions clearly and concisely
				5. Adjusting to group and individual response and stimulating participation when it seems warranted
				6. Managing time
				7. Being able to interpret and implement a Red Cross course design involving the integration of course content, method, and materials
				8. Assessing whether participants are achieving the course learning objectives
				9. Summarizing or facilitating the summation of discussions and tasks
				10. Making and accepting supporting remarks (interventions) that facilitate learning
				11. Bridging effectively—moving from one topic to another
				12. Wrapping up—summarizing at vantage points in the course, such as at the conclusion of a planning objective
				13. Being aware of my personal attributes that add or detract from my other instructor skills (dress, mannerisms, eye contact, body movement, etc.) and affect learning

For team teaching, the self-assessment should be used in precourse preparations. Identify three (3) skills that you want to improve during the instruction of the course, and with which the co-instructor agrees to give you support.

For other self-development, prepare a development planning worksheet, to include—		
OBJECTIVES	PLAN FOR ACCOMPLISHING	RESOURCES

American Red Cross Form 5898-J (Rev. 5-88)

An example of a plan follows:

Objectives	Plan for Accomplishing	Resources
Managing time	● Determine length of time for each section of material.	Instructor's manual
	● Review block plan.	Block plan
	● Review lesson plan for organization of content.	Lesson plan
	● Determine beginning and ending time.	Clock
	● Have co-instructor give time cue, e.g., "five more minutes."	Co-instructor

Block Plan—Sample

Water Safety Instructor Course

Course purpose: The purpose of this course is to provide the instructor candidate with the knowledge, skill, and teaching know-how to function effectively as a Red Cross Water Safety instructor.

Day 1 (3.5 hrs.)
Introduction
Paperwork
Course overview
Sale of materials
Physical laws
Analysis of swimming
Introduction to Red Cross programs

Day 2 (3.5 hrs.)
Evaluation of crawl, elementary back stroke, breaststroke, sidestroke, and back crawl
Reciprocal teaching of strokes as needed

Day 3 (3.5 hrs.)
Quiz
Understanding of learning process
Methods of teaching
Course management
Stroke evaluation
Inverted breaststroke
Lifesaving review

Day 4 (3.5 hrs.)
Beginner swimmer skills
Stroke evaluation
Trudgen stroke
Overarm sidestroke
Lifesaving films
Teaching the beginner swimmer
Lifesaving review

Day 5 (3.5 hrs.)   Quiz
Lifesaving films
Final exam for swimmer skills
Practice teaching
Lifesaving review
Stroke practice

Day 6 (3.5 hrs.)   Red Cross swimming classes
Red Cross lifesaving program
Red Cross leadership program
Lifesaving films
Lifesaving teaching techniques
Practice teaching
Lifesaving skill evaluation
Stroke evaluation

Day 7 (5.5 hrs.)   Review for written final
Lifesaving practice teaching
Artificial respiration
Mask, fin, and snorkel
Lost bather's team
Neck and back injuries
Small craft
Paddle board
First aid

Day 8 (3 hrs.)   Final written exam
Skill evaluation—lifesaving and swimming
Practice teaching

Day 9 (3 hrs.)   Review written exam
Red Cross orientation
Course Record forms
Authorization forms
Responsibilities as a Red Cross
  Water Safety instructor
  Future opportunities

SAMPLE LESSON PLAN

TIME	CONTENT	ACTIVITY	RESOURCES
	1. Values clarification		
	The purpose of this session is to summarize concepts and to explain the function of values clarification as an approach for facilitating classroom communication and as a set of methods for teaching health.		Handout 25, Values Clarification
	2. Definitions	Presentation with transparencies	Transparencies 29, 30, 31, 32
	a. Values		
	Things that people hold worthy and that have merit or importance in their lives		
	b. Values clarification		
	1. The process of examining values		
	2. The use of learning strategies to help people clarify their own values		
	3. Process of valuing	Transparency on the valuing process	Transparency 30
	Louis Raths developed the theory on the process of valuing. He identified the following steps in the process:		
	a. Prizing		
	1. Cherishing, being happy with the choice		
	2. Publicly affirming the choice, when applicable		

SAMPLE LESSON PLAN

TIME	CONTENT	ACTIVITY	RESOURCES
	b. Choosing		
	The choice should be made—		
	1. Freely.		
	2. From alternatives.		
	3. After thoughtful consideration of the consequences.		
	c. Acting		
	1. Doing something with the choice		
	2. Acting repeatedly in a consistent pattern		
	4. Influences on the development of values	Ask the participants to think of a personal experience involving the process of valuing. Ask individuals to share their experiences as appropriate and as time permits.	
	a. Parents, families		
	b. Media		
	c. Culture		
	d. Friends, peer group		
	e. Government	Develop this list of influences on blank newsprint.	Newsprint
	f. Religion		

126

The Five Key Commitments

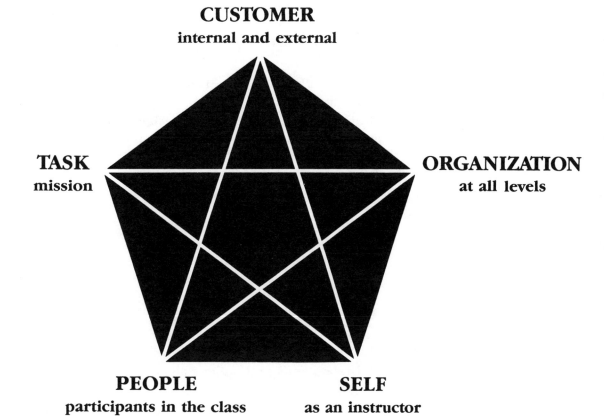

CUSTOMER
internal and external

TASK
mission

ORGANIZATION
at all levels

PEOPLE
participants in the class

SELF
as an instructor

Five Key Commitments

Commitment to the Customer

The Excellent Instructor:
- Knows that the ultimate external customer receives service.
- Clearly communicates this importance to all participants.
- Does not allow destructive comments about the people we serve.
- Recognizes that customers are served best by well-trained workers.
- Knows that participants and their units are the internal customers.
- Emphasizes the importance of excellent service delivery.
- Is dedicated to providing participants the best possible training.

Commitment to the Organization

The Excellent Instructor:
- Understands and supports the organization and its management.
- Discourages destructive comments about the organization.
- Is honest and positive in describing organizational programs.
- Inspires pride in the organization and the service.
- Supports higher level management decisions by challenging up and supporting down.
- Does not "pass the buck" or blame others in the organization.
- Understands and operates by the basic values of the organization.
- Encourages others to perform to high standards and values.

Commitment to the Task

The Excellent Instructor:
- Thoroughly prepares for every training assignment.
- Knows and supports the mission of the organization.
- Understands and can interpret policies, regulations, and procedures.
- Concentrates on participant achievement so course learning can take place.

- Provides a climate in which effective learning can take place.
- Makes presentations so that they can be understood and implemented.
- Makes the training meaningful and relevant to participants.

Commitment to People

The Excellent Instructor:

- Consistently shows respect and concern for people as individuals.
- Effectively analyzes individual and group performance.
- Gives timely and corrective developmental and performance feedback.
- Gives participants positive recognition for achievement.
- Avoids destructive comments about people or their performance.
- Provides opportunities for participants to test their learning.
- Responds to questions in a timely and effective manner.

Commitment to Self

The Excellent Instructor:

- Is dedicated to continued personal development as an instructor.
- Takes responsibility for the accomplishment of learning objectives.
- Demonstrates confidence in ability as an instructor.
- Is willing to admit and correct mistakes.
- Encourages and accepts constructive advice or criticism.
- Shows a high degree of personal integrity.
- Blends autonomy and teamwork into effective team teaching.

Managing Diversity to Enhance the Learning Process

What is diversity? Diversity is the quality or condition of being different from one another. The many differences among people include gender, race, ethnicity, religion, physical disabilities or impairments, language, sexual orientation, age, socioeconomic background, educational experiences, and work experiences to name a few.

For complete information on Red Cross guidelines concerning the subject of diversity, see the American Red Cross *Legal Resources Manual* (ARC 4504), Chapter 8, Section II. The guidelines listed below concern the issue of diversity in the classroom and are taken from the *Health and Safety Manual of Administrative Policies and Procedures* (ARC 3530), Section VII-5.

In the performance of its manifold humanitarian services, the policy and practice of the American Red Cross has been and continues to be based on fundamental concepts that—

- No person shall be deprived of Red Cross service because of his or her color, sex, race, religious beliefs, national origin, or physical or mental handicap as described in the Rehabilitation Act of 1973, except where any individual's safety will, in the opinion of the Red Cross, be adversely affected by the participation of a disabled individual in a Red Cross course.

- There shall be no segregation on the basis of such criteria in facilities owned, leased, or controlled by the Red Cross.

- No person shall be deprived of Red Cross service because of his or her inability to pay.

- The Red Cross will not knowingly sponsor or conduct services or program activities intended for the general public in facilities controlled by others unless such services or program activities are conducted in a manner consistent with these Red Cross principles.

Some suggestions for handling diversity in the classroom follow.

Planning to Teach

As you prepare to teach your course, learn as much as you can about your participants. This can be done in several ways. The course registrations or applications, if used, give you some demographic data. Also, talking with representatives of the sponsoring Red Cross unit may give you some additional insights. Learn what you can about the course participants, including their—

- Gender, race, ethnicity, culture, age.
- Educational experience (formal and informal).
- Job responsibilities.
- Language abilities.
- Physical attributes.
- Other factors that might affect the learning process.

Based on the mix of the course participants, discuss with both your co-instructor and the sponsoring unit any areas that are particularly sensitive. Also discuss how any issues and media coverage of issues that have divided or united the community recently affect the classroom situation.

Once you have some general information on how the course participants differ, find out as much as you can about how these differences affect learning preferences. Before the course begins, gather, if possible, information about cultural norms as they relate to learning by—

- Asking the sponsoring unit about observations of or feedback from course participants in previous training experiences.

- Talking with people you know who share the same cultural background as the course participants about educational practices within their culture.

- Obtaining information about the training methods with which participants from diverse cultures are most comfortable, e.g., individual work, small group work, lecture, discussion. (Also try to determine how they view their role and the role of instructors. Do they prefer to communicate with each other or with the instructors?)

Participants for whom the course language is challenging may appreciate receiving relevant materials to allow time for review before a course begins. (In some instances, American Red Cross course materials have been translated into a language that may be easier for some participants to understand. Check first with the Red Cross unit sponsoring the course for information about translations. Furthermore, some Red Cross units can provide a translator for the class.)

Conducting the Course

During the climate setting phase of the course, tell the participants that you and the Red Cross value diversity and believe that diversity is a positive enhancement to the learning environment. As part of setting the climate, acknowledge the diversity that exists in the classroom and stress that each of us comes to class with his or her own history, frame of reference, unique experiences, and ideas from which we can all share and learn. Emphasize that this diversity is part of what makes learning rich, interesting, and exciting.

During the course introduction, tell the participants about the teaching methods that will be used. Explain that you will attempt to incorporate methods that you hope will match their learning preferences. Be honest about how your teaching methods may not coincide with everyone's learning preferences. Explain the benefits of the methods that are used in the course, and offer to provide extra support to those who are unfamiliar with these teaching methods.

While teaching the course, be consistent in your acknowledgment and feedback. Apply the same standards of evaluation to all participants unless the rigid application of those standards would result in unfair treatment to a particular group of people.

In a group with diverse language abilities, check often for comprehension. One method of checking is to ask participants to tell you what they understand about the current topic in their own words. By asking a few participants at a time, you will receive feedback from all participants over the duration of the course. Maintain a normal voice pitch and speaking pace with all participants. It is not unusual to assume that speaking loudly to those with an accent or to those who are challenged by the language of the course will improve their comprehension. This is not true. Also, it is not valid to assume that a participant with an accent will have trouble comprehending.

Decide in advance how you will structure learning activities within the course design to maximize opportunities for inclusion of all participants, but be aware of possible discomfort that may be created when certain course activities are in conflict with cultural norms. Some examples include—

- Participation in role-playing for a person who is more comfortable with a highly instructive approach.
- Participation in group discussions or presentations by another participant from a culture where instructors are viewed as the expert.
- Attending courses that are predominately lecture for persons who are used to a participative learning environment.

Remember it is counterproductive to force anyone to participate in activities that cause undue discomfort, as this may block learning. While you may not be able to change dramatically the way you teach your course, you can be sensitive to cues that learning is not taking place. Participants may show the following cues indicating that they are not learning:

- Withdrawal
- Distraction
- Aggressive behavior
- Defensiveness
- Visibly upset

In all teaching settings, avoid ethnic or sexual jokes. Do not make jokes or remarks that belittle others. Avoid using slang, sarcasm, exaggerations, idioms, and puns as they are often misinterpreted. Also avoid negative remarks about yourself, the Red Cross or others. Remember that sometimes a word, remark, comment, or some type of nonverbal behavior made by you, the co-instructor, or another participant causes a participant or several participants to be distracted from the learning process. The words or behaviors may not be intended to be offensive or insensitive, but they may result in perceptions causing discomfort to some participants.

Sometimes you will hear or see the troublesome words or behaviors and the verbal or nonverbal response of others, but sometimes you will not. You may become aware that some situation has occurred because you recognize that learning has been blocked. Whether you hear or observe the distracting words or behaviors or you have picked up on the cues, you need to respond to the situation.

Offensive behavior or improper word choice must be dealt with to get the learning back on track. How you deal with the situation requires a great deal of care and sensitivity on your part. You will need to make decisions about how and when the issue will be addressed and who will be included in the discussion.

In such situations, some basic human relations principles to which instructors can adhere are to—

- Focus on the situation, issue, or behavior—not on the individual.

- Maintain the self-esteem and self-confidence of everyone by not making statements that belittle anyone or cause any embarrassment.

- Deal with issues quickly and clearly; avoid belaboring them.

- Remain professional, using a sensitive and caring tone and being careful not to pass judgment or lay blame.

- Check, with others if necessary, to make certain your assumptions are correct.

- State what you have observed or seen and how you are feeling.

- View the situation as an opportunity to help participants become aware of people who are different from them and include them in the learning group.

- Keep in mind, "What can I do to maintain an open, positive, learning climate?"

- Communicate sincerely and honestly.

These recommendations, though helpful, may not solve all issues that block learning. Some issues may need to be discussed during a class break, or after class. In some situations, you may need to involve the course sponsor for follow-up.

Participant Resources

**Participant
Resource 1:**   General Outline

**Participant
Resource 2:**   Purpose, Objectives, and Criteria for Completion

**Participant
Resource 3:**   Crossword Puzzle

**Participant
Resource 4:**   Nonverbal Communication

**Participant
Resource 5:**   Feedback Exercise

**Participant
Resource 6:**   Assigning Group Tasks

**Participant
Resource 7:**   Evaluations, Records, and Reports Form

**Participant
Resource 8:**   American Red Cross Instructor Candidate Training Participant
Reaction Form

**Participant
Resource 9:**   American Red Cross Instructor Candidate Training Answer Sheet

General Outline (Unit 1)

Unit Titles		Time Frame
Unit 1	Introducing the Course	35 minutes
Unit 2	Understanding Students and the	
	Learning Process	35 minutes
Break		10 minutes
Unit 3	Being an Effective Instructor	55 minutes
Unit 4	Conducting a Course–Part I	45 minutes
	First Session Total (3 hours)	180 minutes
Break	(Lunch or end of Day 1)	
Unit 4	Conducting a Course–Part II	50 minutes
Unit 5	Completing Evaluations, Records,	
	and Reports	30 minutes
Break		10 minutes
Unit 6	Planning to Teach	20 minutes
Unit 7	Representing the Red Cross	35 minutes
Unit 8	Course Summary and Evaluation	35 minutes
	Second Session Total (3 hours)	180 minutes

Purpose, Objectives, and Criteria for Completion (Unit 1)

Course Purpose The purpose of this course is to provide training for entry-level instructor candidates, to enable cross training to occur more readily between services, and to better accommodate instructor training in local units.

Course Objectives By the end of the course, the participant should be able to—
- Describe factors that enhance learning.
- Identify instructor functions.
- Describe teaching methods common to Red Cross courses.
- Describe the rationale for evaluation in Red Cross courses.
- Explain the need for accurate, timely reporting and record keeping.
- Describe steps in planning to teach.
- Explain the importance of representing the Red Cross effectively.

Criteria for Course Completion The criteria for successful completion of this course are meeting the objectives through—
- Attendance at all sessions.
- A passing score of 80 percent or higher on the written test.
- Participation in task assignments and other activities.

Crossword Puzzle (Unit 2)

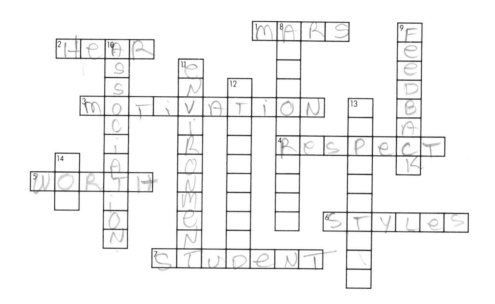

ACROSS

1. The mnemonic for the four concepts used in learning is _____.

2. _____, see, and do should be kept in mind when trying to maximize the use of senses.

3. What the "M" in MARS stands for.

4. Recognition and _____ of the student are important ingredients in maintaining a supportive climate, and, therefore, motivation.

5. In order to be motivated, students must understand the _____ of the subject.

6. The more senses we use when teaching helps to meet students' different learning _____.

7. Understanding and applying "MARS" will help the _____ learn.

DOWN

8. Students who are engaged with the course material at the _____ difficulty level will have a better chance of being motivated to learn.

9. Students must receive prompt corrective _____, so that they can correct mistakes.

10. The use of examples based on students' experience is using the concept of _____.

11. Lighting, temperature, and acoustics in the classroom are factors of the _____ that may affect motivation.

12. _____ practice rather than unstructured practice promotes repetition.

13. Review of material and structured practice are elements in the concept of _____.

14. A reason or motivation for taking a course might be that it is required by one's _____.

Nonverbal Communication (Unit 3)

Directions: Partner A reads the statement below. Next, Partner B describes the body language used and the perceived meaning of the nonverbal communication. Partner B describes the effect on learning.

Note: Partner A speaks clearly and distinctly but with an arrogant-sounding voice. Examples of nonverbal communication to use are—pointing at Partner B, raising the eyebrows, sitting stiffly with the chin thrust upward, etc., indicating an air of superiority.

Statement: "When soliciting a major gift from a financial donor, it is important to plan carefully. Selecting the person who will be soliciting the gift is critical. Although the procedure states that it should be done in person, I believe that people with as much experience as I have could do an excellent job of soliciting by telephone."

Nonverbal Communication (Unit 3)

Directions: Partner B reads the statement below. Next, Partner A describes the body language used and the perceived meaning of the nonverbal communication. Partner A describes the effect on learning.

Note: Partner B speaks in a monotone and mumbles words and uses body language indicating there is little interest in the subject. For example, slump in the chair, figet, and keep head down, avoiding direct eye contact, etc.

Statement: "When soliciting a major gift from a financial donor, it is important to plan carefully. Selecting the person who will solicit the gift is crucial. This should always be done in person and by an individual who is a peer of the potential donor."

Feedback Exercise (Unit 3)

Situation I   You are teaching a Disaster Services course. You have given written directions for a "pair exercise," in which one student is to play the disaster victim, and the other student is to play the Red Cross volunteer. The purpose of the exercise is to practice conducting an interview.

As you check to see how the pair is progressing with the exercise, you see that the "client" is showing the "interviewer" the role information on the handout. Consequently, the "interviewer" is not interviewing the "victim," which is one of the purposes of the exercise.

In your exact words, provide the corrective feedback to the pair.

(Please record below your corrective feedback for Situation I.)

Situation II   You are teaching How to Measure Blood Pressure, a Health and Safety course. The student is practicing inflating a blood pressure cuff wrapped around a coffee can. As you watch, you see that the student is squeezing the bulb to pump up the cuff, and you hear a hissing sound. The hissing means that the valve is open (the valve screw has not been turned all the way to the right to close it). The cuff cannot be inflated properly.

In your own words, provide the corrective feedback to the student.

(Please record below your corrective feedback for Situation II.)

Assigning Group Tasks (Unit 4)

Directions: In your task groups, appoint a member who will report your group's conclusions to the class. Discuss the following questions:

1. As an instructor, what are the steps you would follow in assigning a task to a group? Sequence the steps in the order in which they would normally occur.

2. What points did you learn from the video segment on task groups that you feel will help you be a more effective instructor?

Evaluations, Records, and Reports Form (Unit 5)

Directions: Place an "X" in the column that provides the data for the listed use.

Uses of Data	Course Record	Participant Reaction Form	Instructor Reaction Form
Validates that course was held.			
Gives data for community fund raising.			
Documents instructor's activities/performance.			
Provides data for recruiting for the course.			
Provides data for improving your teaching performance.			
Documents certification process.			
Provides data to improve course administration.			
Provides data to reauthorize instructor.			
Provides data on whether participants liked the course.			
Provides statistical data for reports to community and national sector.			
Provides data for revising the course by the national sector.			

Instructor Trainer 1 _____

Instructor Trainer 2 _____

Date _____

American Red Cross
Instructor Candidate Training
Participant Reaction Form

We would like to know what you thought about this American Red Cross course. Please circle your answer.

	Very Effective	Effective	Not Sure	Not Effective	N/A
I. Content Evaluation: How effective was this course in explaining—					
the 4 steps in the Red Cross instructor training process?	1	2	3	4	❏
ways to help students learn?	1	2	3	4	❏
the 5 instructor functions, i.e., BASIC?	1	2	3	4	❏
student characteristics that might affect learning?	1	2	3	4	❏
instructor characteristics that enhance learning?	1	2	3	4	❏
teaching methods common to Red Cross courses?	1	2	3	4	❏
evaluation strategies used by the Red Cross?	1	2	3	4	❏
the planning required to teach a Red Cross course?	1	2	3	4	❏
the Red Cross and its mission, programs, and services.	1	2	3	4	❏

	Strongly Agree	Agree	Not Sure	Dis-agree	N/A
II. Instructor Trainer Effectiveness					
The instructor trainer was well prepared and organized.					
Instructor Trainer 1	1	2	3	4	❏
Instructor Trainer 2	1	2	3	4	❏
The information was explained clearly.					
Instructor Trainer 1	1	2	3	4	❏
Instructor Trainer 2	1	2	3	4	❏

	Strongly Agree	Agree	Not Sure	Dis-agree	N/A
II. Instructor Trainer Effectiveness (cont)					
The instructor trainer helped me learn.					
Instructor Trainer 1	1	2	3	4	❑
Instructor Trainer 2	1	2	3	4	❑
The instructor trainer involved the class in discussions and exercises.					
Instructor Trainer 1	1	2	3	4	❑
Instructor Trainer 2	1	2	3	4	❑
The instructor trainer answered my questions clearly					
Instructor Trainer 1	1	2	3	4	❑
Instructor Trainer 2	1	2	3	4	❑
III. Overall Course Evaluation					
The course was well paced.	1	2	3	4	❑
The use of instructional aids helped me learn. (i.e., videos, transparencies, posters, etc.)	1	2	3	4	❑
The test questions covered important content in the course.	1	2	3	4	❑
I now feel better prepared to become a Red Cross instructor.	1	2	3	4	❑

OVERALL I WOULD RATE THIS COURSE AS:

Excellent   Good   Average   Below Average   Poor

What did you like most about the course?

_____

What did you like least about the course?

_____

Please share any specific comments about this course or your instructor trainer(s) on an additional sheet of paper and attach to this form.

If you would like us to contact you for any reason, please include your name and phone number.

Name _____ Daytime Phone Number (   ) _____

THANK YOU FOR ANSWERING THESE QUESTIONS. WE HOPE YOU ENJOYED THE COURSE.

Signature (optional) _____

American Red Cross Instructor Candidate Training Answer Sheet

Name: _____   Test: _____ A _____ B

Directions: Darken the circle containing the letter for the correct answer for each question.

1. (a)(b)(c)(d)   14. (a)(b)(c)(d)
2. (a)(b)(c)(d)   15. (a)(b)(c)(d)
3. (a)(b)(c)(d)   16. (a)(b)(c)(d)
4. (a)(b)(c)(d)   17. (a)(b)(c)(d)
5. (a)(b)(c)(d)   18. (a)(b)(c)(d)
6. (a)(b)(c)(d)   19. (a)(b)(c)(d)
7. (a)(b)(c)(d)   20. (a)(b)(c)(d)
8. (a)(b)(c)(d)   21. (a)(b)(c)(d)
9. (a)(b)(c)(d)   22. (a)(b)(c)(d)
10. (a)(b)(c)(d)   23. (a)(b)(c)(d)
11. (a)(b)(c)(d)   24. (a)(b)(c)(d)
12. (a)(b)(c)(d)   25. (a)(b)(c)(d)
13. (a)(b)(c)(d)

You may wish to go back and check your answers to be sure that you matched the right answer with the right question.